ADMISSIONS GUIDE TO SELECTIVE BUSINESS SCHOOLS

Matthew May

VGM Career Horizons
a division of *NTC Publishing Group*
Lincolnwood, Illinois USA

To my father and mother, without whose constant love and support I'd have never made it this far. . . .

Library of Congress Cataloging-in-Publication Data

May, Matthew, 1959–
   Admissions guide to selective business schools.

   1. Business schools—United States—Admission.
2. Master of business administration degree—United States.   I. Title.
HF1131.M3547   1990   650'.071'173   90-12199
ISBN 0-8442-8550-1
ISBN 0-8442-8556-0 (pbk.)

1992 Printing

Published by VGM Career Horizons, a division of NTC Publishing Group.
© 1990 by NTC Publishing Group, 4255 West Touhy Avenue,
Lincolnwood (Chicago), Illinois 60646-1975 U.S.A.
All rights reserved. No part of this book may be reproduced, stored
in a retrieval system, or transmitted in any form or by any means,
electronic, mechanical, photocopying, recording or otherwise, without
the prior permission of NTC Publishing Group.
Manufactured in the United States of America.

   2 3 4 5 6 7 8 9 VP 9 8 7 6 5 4 3 2

CONTENTS

Introduction vii
Why a Book About Business School Applications?
Who Should Use This Book?
What Is in This Book?
Part I
Part II
Part III

Part I The Marketplace 1
Part I at a Glance

1 The Realities of the Marketplace 3

2 The Nation's Top Business Schools 7

3 Trends in the Top Business Schools 13

Part II The Competition 17
Part II at a Glance

4 Admissions Committees 19
Who Are They?
How Will They Decide Your Case?

5 The Competitive Candidate 25
What Are Admissions Committees Looking for?

6 What Makes a Successful Application? 28
OBJECTIVE CRITERIA
How Much Work Experience Is Needed?
What Kinds Are Best?
How Important Are Undergraduate Grades?
How Important Are GMAT Scores?
How Important Are Extracurricular Activities?
How Important Are Letters of Reference?
SUBJECTIVE CRITERIA
How Important Are the Personal Essays?
How Important Are Interviews?
Applications That Committees Dread
A Few Things to Consider Before You Begin

**Part III   The Strategy—Beating
the Competition** 41
Part III at a Glance

7 The Essays—How to Present Yourself 43
What Does the Committee Want to Hear?
What You Must Convey About Yourself and How to Say It
Essay Writing Strategy and the Writing Process
How to Address the Different Types of Essay Questions

"You, the MBA, and Your Career"
"Substantial Achievements or Accomplishments"
"Leadership and Responsibility"
"Self-Analysis"
"Ethical Dilemmas"
"For Fun"
Other Essay Types

8 Letters of Reference 108
Whom Should You Ask to Recommend You?
What Should a Good Reference Letter Say?
How to Make a Recommendation Request

9 Acing the GMAT 118
What Is the GMAT?
How Is the GMAT Scored?
Preparation, Strategy, and Commonly Asked Questions

10 The Interview—A New Feature 143
Should You Seek an Interview Even if It's Not Required?
What Types of Interviews Exist at Present?
How Should You Prepare for the Interview?
What Are Some Guidelines You Should Follow?
What Kinds of Questions Can You Expect?

11 Once You're In 155

Appendix A: Application File Tracker 159

Appendix B: Letter of Recommendation
             Organizer 160
Appendix C: Relevant Reading Material 162
Appendix D: Personal Data File 163

INTRODUCTION

Why a Book About Business School Applications?

There was a time, and not so very long ago, when applying to a graduate school of business was a reasonably straightforward process. In those halcyon days, the prospective MBA, usually a college senior, would research a reference guide or two, register to take the Graduate Management Admissions Test (GMAT), and then apply to a few schools. The application consisted of a single personal statement, a reference letter or two, and an undergraduate transcript. This scenario was familiar as recently as the late 1970s but seems antediluvian given today's admissions climate.

Now it is virtually impossible for a college senior lacking in full-time work experience to enter a top business school directly from college, and the one-page personal statement has been replaced by as many as 13 self-analytical, introspective essay questions. Being admitted to a top business school is no easy feat—in fact, it's the toughest part of getting an "elite MBA." Every prospective MBA needs an understanding of the complex and nebulous nature of the present-day admissions process at the nation's most selective business schools—it is the key that unlocks ivy-shrouded doors of schools like Harvard and Wharton. This book was written to meet the needs of all prospective MBAs.

Who Should Use This Book?

This book is designed to be used as a complete strategic device for gaining admission to selective MBA programs *once you've made the decision to apply to graduate business school.*

In order to derive the maximum benefit from this book, you should be fully committed to pursuing an MBA and presently be at the application stage of the admissions process. This book does *not* purport to be an informational guide to MBA programs. It should be used as neither a career decision-making tool nor an aid in deciding whether one should consider pursuing an MBA. These are personal choices. Additionally, many books already exist on these topics and may be consulted first.

If you have made a *firm* decision to get your MBA, and are now attempting to gain acceptance to the school(s) of your choice, then this book is for you.

What Is in This Book?

This book is designed to be a business plan (not coincidentally, and quite appropriately) for gaining admission to the business school of your choice. It takes you through the entire application process to acceptance at a top MBA program. Step-by-step, it tells you what to do and how to do it, making the process of admission as clear and as straightforward as possible. Part I of the book (Chapters 1–3) addresses the current state of affairs with respect to top business schools and their programs and admissions. Part II (Chapters 4–6) describes the necessary ingredients of a successful application and unlocks some of the secrets surrounding admissions committees. Part III (Chapters 7–10) forms the heart of the book. It describes exactly how to prepare an effective and well-written application in order to maximize the probability of acceptance.

If you already have begun to examine applications of schools to which you will apply, you may want to skim Part I; read Part II; and use Part III as a desktop reference source as you write your applications.

Part I–The Marketplace

The information in Part I provides background.

Chapter 1 begins by discussing the nature of the MBA "name game" and explains the importance of receiving an MBA from a nationally ranked business school.

Chapter 2 provides a description and comparison of the schools commonly thought of as being in the Top Ten. It provides the reader with a quick inside look at some of the better schools and, to some extent, elaborates on the basic differences and similarities within the top-tier schools.

Chapter 3 brings the reader up-to-date with respect to the current trends in the admissions policies and curricula of the top schools, focusing on the most recent developments.

Part II—The Competition

In Part II, the discussion focuses on the admissions process and the components of the application.

Chapter 4 sheds light on the decision-making process of admissions committees and provides insight into the committees themselves.

Chapter 5 explores the "ideal" candidate and discusses those qualities most sought after in an applicant, from an admissions officer's viewpoint.

Chapter 6 gives an in-depth look at the various components of a successful application (essays, work experience, GMAT scores, letters of reference) and their relative importance and contribution to the whole. The chapter ends by offering practical tips for getting started on the applications.

Part III—The Strategy

In Part III, the applicant receives a guided step-by-step tour through preparing the very best application possible.

Chapter 7 covers the most important component of the application—the essays. The applicant learns essay strategy: what is expected, how to begin the writing process, and "do's and don'ts." In addition, each type of essay is thoroughly dissected and the "hidden questions" illuminated.

Chapter 8 focuses on reference letter strategy: how to secure the very best letters, what determines a good letter, who should write the letters, and how to approach potential recommenders.

Chapter 9 describes a general approach to preparing for the Graduate Management Admissions Test. Test-taking strategies and tips for acing the test are given as well.

Chapter 10 focuses on a relatively new addition to the admissions process—the personal interview. Typical interview questions are described, and appropriate responses are outlined.

Chapter 11 concludes the strategy section and gives suggestions for properly weighing business school options once the applicant has been accepted.

PART ONE

■

THE MARKETPLACE

Part I at a Glance

This section of the book will provide a brief look at the reasons behind pursuing an MBA at the top business schools in the nation. A short look at who comprises the top tier of schools will be given, followed by a quick synopsis of the recent trends in curricula and admissions at these schools.

1

The Realities of the Marketplace

Recruiter: "I've got three candidates that I think will be perfect for the job."

Executive: "Tell me a bit about them."

Recruiter: "Well, as you know, they're all recent MBAs. One is from Harvard, one is from Wharton, and the third is from Oregon State."

Executive: "Tell you what, let's just interview the Harvard and Wharton MBAs."

Fair or not, the above dialogue indicates the harsh reality that faces the tens of thousands of newly minted MBAs each year. The most lucrative and prestigious jobs go to the Harvard and Wharton MBAs of the world. The fact of the matter is that the employment market for MBAs is a "name game" at the major league level, and an MBA from one of the elite graduate schools of business in the country has a front-row ticket. This book is devoted to the successful pursuit of the elite MBA.

Dean Russell Palmer of The Wharton School, one of the leading MBA programs in the nation, was once quoted as saying, "Today the MBA doesn't mean that much. Today it's where you get it." This is the reality of the marketplace. The reasons behind this reality stem from the simple economics of supply and demand. There is a glut on the market of graduates with MBAs, and the demand for those with MBAs is, in general, slackening.

In 1987, graduate schools of business in America granted as many MBAs as were graduated during the entire decade of the 1960s. The total number of programs has skyrocketed as well. Fifteen years ago, there were just over 300 full-time MBA programs in existence; now there are over 650. The reasons behind this enormous growth aren't easily pinpointed. At the root, however, is the desire of the corporate community to identify those outstanding individuals who should be groomed for top business management positions. Years ago, this was done by observation of on-the-job performance. As corporations grew in size, diversification, and bureaucracy, this individual progress observation and attention became less and less feasible. The next credential used to identify potential managers was the four-year college degree. But as a significantly greater proportion of the population earned college degrees, the degree alone was not selective enough, and so the Masters of Business Administration gradually became the predictor of managerial success. Now, with so many MBAs flooding the job market, that too is no longer selective enough. Now, as Dean

Palmer says, it's where you go for your MBA. Not only is an MBA needed to advance beyond middle management positions in today's executive ladder, but you need an MBA from one of the "right" schools—the nation's top five or 10 graduate schools of business. While the overall demand for MBAs is down, the demand for graduates of the top schools by corporations, consulting firms, investment houses, and entrepreneurial ventures continues to grow unabated. Thus, it is more important than ever to get an MBA from a top school. These elite programs are able to protect and ensure this great demand for their graduates by wisely and purposely limiting the size of their entering classes. This creates incredibly stiff competition for available spots and maintains the quality and integrity of the schools' reputation.

The demand for graduates of the top business schools is reflected in the recent starting salaries offered by employers. *Average* annual starting salaries of graduates from the top ten schools are rapidly approaching $60,000. "Star" salaries, offered to graduates of these schools with either particularly strong previous work experience or who graduate near the top of their class, can exceed $100,000 with bonuses and other perks. More typical starting salaries approach $75,000 for investment banking, $80,000 for management consulting, $55,000 for general management, and $45,000 for advertising. Signing bonuses, not unlike those received by professional athletes, can be as much as 30 percent of the starting salary. These figures are as much as $30,000 per year more than what graduates of schools with lesser reputations are offered. This "sweet smell of success" is certainly another motivating reason to attend one of the elite business schools.

Employers easily justify such high starting salaries by noting that graduates of these most selective programs move up the corporate ladder more quickly, take responsibility and command more effectively, and bring with them to the job a far superior blend of intelligence, skills, and confidence. Their abilities and skills have been improved and expanded through training using the latest management techniques, technology, theory, and practice. An unbelievably large percentage of America's business tycoons, corporate presidents, and chief executive officers are graduates of the top business schools. While these business leaders (such as Donald Trump, a Wharton alumnus) would in all probability have made it eventually to the top of their respective fields no matter what their educational background, it is safe to say that their formal business education facilitated their rise to success.

Anyone seriously considering the Master of Business Administration cannot ignore the realities of the competitive employment marketplace. Neither can one ignore the enormous advantage gained over the rest of the market by graduating from one of the nation's top-tier MBA programs. Since only a handful of business schools have the prestige to realistically grant this edge, it stands to reason that great difficulty and stiff competition exist for the limited number of available spots in the entering classes of these schools. Thus, the goal then becomes one of gaining admission to one of these programs. This is the most difficult part of getting your MBA from a prestigious business school, but it *can* be done. As a first step in the process, however, we must identify those MBA programs that are considered to be the best in the nation.

2

The Nation's Top Business Schools

Kellogg. Wharton. Harvard. Stanford. Chicago. Sloan. Tuck. Columbia. UCLA. Michigan. These are thought to be the nation's most elite MBA programs—the best of the select—followed closely by Berkeley, Colgate-Darden, Carnegie-Mellon, Cornell, Indiana, Fuqua, and Yale. It's difficult, and probably pointless, to try to identify the number one school in the country. Traditionally, Harvard, Stanford, and Wharton have shared top honors. A *Business Week* article of November 1988 ranked Kellogg as number one, followed by Wharton and Harvard. A 1985 Brecker & Merryman survey duplicated this top tier. The *Jack Gourman Report* rates Harvard as number one, with Wharton and Stanford in close pursuit. Picking the one top business school in the country is akin to identifying the best automobile in the world—you can identify five top models, but the *best?* It depends on who is doing the rating.

The differences between the top schools are, for the most part, minor. True, Harvard's case method teaching approach is diametrically opposed to Chicago's theoretical approach. Most of the top ten schools, though, differ primarily in personality, reputation, and location. Kellogg, Amos Tuck, and Cornell are known for the comraderie that exists between and among students and faculty. Harvard is just the opposite—the 800 cases to read and the military school mentality foster a much different, more alienated environment. Colgate-Darden adheres to the same approach and is fast becoming the "Harvard of the South." Stanford and Wharton seem to be a mix of the two extremes: friendly competition and a fun time within a rigorous curriculum. Chicago, Sloan, and Carnegie-Mellon are the masters of the number-crunching approach—if you're a quantitative person, you'll fit in well at these schools. What makes Columbia and UCLA stand apart is their flexibility and geographic location—the Big Apple and the City of Angels. Each has its own distinct culture to offer the student. Michigan, in its down-home environment, takes a down-to-earth, nononsense, no-frills approach to the MBA. Yale, a school that offers an MPPM (Masters in Public and Private Management) rather than an MBA, stands apart if only for this very aspect of the curriculum. One thing is certain: You can't go wrong by attending any one of these top schools. More important to realize is that the better schools have more in common with each other than they do differences between them.

What can the prospective MBA expect from the nation's best business schools? The list is a long one that would include the following: •A supportive and cooperative learning environment that will encourage you to broaden your education as well as challenge you intellectually. •A top-notch faculty at the cutting edge of research and technology, inquiring into the issues and problems of today's business. •The best and brightest students, selected for their diversity, intelligence, maturity, and accomplishments. •The opportunity to be a part of academic and social life at a leading institution of higher learning. •A curriculum that is rigorous, flexible, and constantly being updated with the latest developments in business administration and management theory and practice. •A common set of goals, including: providing prospective MBAs with the expertise they need to become effective, professional executives; providing an awareness and understanding of the economic, political, and social environments in which business operates; providing a stimulating forum to promote innovative thinking, recognition of potential problems, and creative problem solving; providing basic analytical skills in all functions and areas of business; developing expertise in applying these skills to problem solving and strategy formulation; strengthening interpersonal skills for effective and productive working relationships; building self-confidence and the capacity to make effective use of experience and skills; and, last but certainly not least, providing employment and career opportunities and life-long contacts.

Additionally, the top schools have recently joined in the belief that prospective MBAs should not overspecialize in any one area of training, even when they are educating students whose careers will be in professional organizations that require and demand a high level of technical expertise. Students' potential at these schools is developed through curricula that cultivate concern for the administration of a total enterprise in a complex and technologically changing environment.

The chart in this chapter briefly compares some of the vital statistics of the top ten or so business schools. It will be up to you as a prospective MBA to fully investigate the catalogs and individual characteristics of the different schools to discover which schools align most with your own personal preferences for graduate education. Many guidebooks exist to aid you in this decision, the titles of which you'll find at the end of this book. *The Official Guide to MBA Programs, Admissions and Careers,* published by the Graduate Management Admissions Council, is probably the most comprehensive of these. This group also sponsors a series of MBA forums throughout the country, in which member schools send representatives to speak with prospective MBA candidates. It's a perfect time to meet admissions officers and ask questions, attend panel discussions, and watch videotaped discussions. It is best, though, if you can find the time to visit the campuses of the schools that interest you. You'll be better able to judge whether you'll fit in if you take the time to interact with the students and faculty when you visit. When all is said and done, however, it is most likely that you'll attend the school with the highest reputation that admits you, and rightly so, for the reasons cited in the first chapter. The remainder of this book will concentrate on achieving the goal of gaining acceptance to the very best school (the one with the best reputation) that you can.

HOW THE TOP SCHOOLS STACK UP

SCHOOL	LOCATION	CLASS SIZE	AVERAGE ENTERING AGE	ANNUAL TUITION	ACCEPTANCE RATE	# OF RECRUITING COMPANIES	AVERAGE STARTING SALARY
KELLOGG	Chicago	500	27	$14,100	20%	300	$53,000
WHARTON	Philadelphia	760	27	$14,300	12%	420	$59,200
HARVARD	Boston	800+	27	$14,250	13%	400	$61,000
U. CHICAGO	Chicago	500	26	$14,500	29%	250	$54,000
U. MICHIGAN	Ann Arbor	415	26	$12,850	33%	338	$45,000
COLUMBIA	New York	725	26	$14,000	30%	325	$49,500
STANFORD	Palo Alto	318	28	$14,100	8%	245	$56,000
UCLA	Los Angeles	391	27	$ 4,806	12%	200	$45,500
AMOS TUCK	Hanover, N.H.	165	26	$14,000	19%	130	$51,100
SLOAN	Boston	185	26	$14,500	22%	160	$52,000

MAJOR INDUSTRIES ENTERED

SCHOOL	FIRST	SECOND	THIRD
KELLOGG	Brand Management (22%)	Finance (21%)	Consulting (15%)
WHARTON	Investments/Finance (18%)	Consulting (15%)	Marketing (10%)
HARVARD	Consulting (30%)	Investments (20%)	Management (18%)
U. CHICAGO	Investments/Finance (24%)	Banking (19%)	Consulting (11%)
U. MICHIGAN	Finance (37%)	Marketing (24%)	Consulting (12%)
COLUMBIA	Investments/Finance (20%)	Banking (20%)	Communications (11%)
STANFORD	Consulting (11%)	Management (10%)	Marketing (10%)
UCLA	Investments/Finance (29%)	Consulting (20%)	Marketing (20%)
AMOS TUCK	Finance (37%)	Consulting (30%)	Marketing (17%)
SLOAN	Finance (31%)	Consulting (26%)	Marketing (17%)

Note: The rankings in these tables are based on the author's findings and opinions.

3

Trends in the Top Business Schools

Harvard has eliminated the Graduate Management Admission Test (GMAT) as an admissions requirement. A minimum of three years work experience before applying to the business school is now the standard. For the first time, evaluative interviews are being conducted as an integral part of the admissions process at a number of top schools. Business schools have come under fire for turning out investment bankers and management consultants rather than much-needed traditional line manufacturing managers. Annual tuition approaches $15,000. Investment by business schools in research, faculty, and facilities is at an all-time high. Personal computers are required of most first-year MBA students, as is working knowledge of popular financial software. "The times, they are a-changin'!"

The rather rapid rate of change in admissions and curricula in the business school upper echelon seems to be fueled by a competition for students driven by the schools themselves. The Wharton School's "Plan for Preeminence" is a case in point. Upon Wharton's Dean Palmer arrival on the scene after stepping down as CEO at the Big Eight accounting firm of Touche Ross, he immediately instituted a several-point plan to make Wharton the premier business school in the world. As an example of but a single step in the direction of academic preeminence, he recently and successfully wooed one of the world's leading financial theorists, Sanford Grossman, away from Princeton for a price no one wishes to discuss. Many other soon-to-be faculty members have been recruited away from other top business schools. The strategy for preeminence also includes a recent and far-reaching plan to internationalize the school, with campuses in Europe and the Far East. And Palmer is just getting started. The result of this competitive investing seems to be a heated race among the top schools not only for world-renowned faculty, but for students as well. The elite schools vie annually for the best and brightest prospective MBAs and actively recruit and court promising young business leaders and entrepreneurs.

The various schools have responded to these stimuli in various ways. Northwestern's Kellogg School, once known for its strength in consumer product marketing, has rounded out its program in much the same way Wharton is now pursuing—by an internationalization of its curriculum to include new international business majors and several attractive foreign exchange and internship programs.

Harvard has reacted to the competition by changing its admission policies. It is hard to determine exactly why Harvard no longer requires the GMAT—it may be to emphasize the school's qualitative problem-solving approach, or simply an attempt (and a very inexpensive one at that) to set itself apart from the rest of the best. Responding to criticism that its graduates, who have been trained to be general managers, enter consulting and banking careers in pursuit of the almighty dollar rather than take lower-paying (initially) general management positions, Harvard has taken a reactive stance by declaring its interest in admitting applicants with line management and manufacturing experience and career aspirations over those espousing banking and consulting as career goals and experience.

The University of Chicago, the nation's leader in the theoretical approach, has taken a lesson from Harvard and the others by following a two-pronged path in response to the competition. First, it has modified its admissions policy from one that only a few years ago accepted the overwhelming majority of the entering class directly from college (work experience was not valued, as the teaching method was and is theoretical in nature rather than by class discussion) to one that now admits only a small percentage of applicants having little or no work experience. Second, it has also rounded out its curriculum by adding many new courses, faculty members, and concentrations, while at the same time instituting new and innovative joint ventures between local institutions and students of the school.

On the West Coast, UCLA's program has improved drastically through donations by John E. Anderson (not coincidentally the new name of the business school)—a brand new multimillion-dollar facility. Too, UCLA has taken a unique approach to its curriculum—students are free to design their own. Second-year consulting projects add to the competitive attractiveness of the school.

There's no question, the top business schools are big business. In the future, applicants can look forward to even more competitive admissions, yet the rewards gained through this interschool competition can only benefit the educational experience and employment outlook of the students. On the other hand, the price to pay is tuition increases of almost 10 percent per year. When compared to the much-improved curricula, facilities, faculty, and increased recruitment resources, this is a relatively small price to pay, and most certainly a worthwhile investment.

We will turn our attention to the task of identifying the admissions process and formulating an approach to getting into these prestigious schools. After all, getting in is the hardest part of getting the MBA!

PART TWO

■

THE COMPETITION

Part II at a Glance

This section of the book is devoted to describing the admission process from an inside perspective and identifying factors that the admissions office will concentrate on in evaluating you as a potential MBA student at their school. Your competition will be identified, setting up the third section of the book, which is devoted to beating the competition. Chapter 4 takes a close inside look at the "secret" workings of admissions committees. Chapter 5 briefly identifies the qualities that have enabled success in gaining admission to top business schools, and Chapter 6 examines the relative importance of the various components making up a business school application.

4

Admissions Committees

In this chapter, we'll examine the inner workings of admissions committees at the selective business schools. The goal of this chapter is simply to enlighten and inform applicants of the process, rather than to suggest second-guessing tactics or providing information to be used in customizing an application.

Who Are They?

When your application folder is complete—essays completed, transcripts received, scores reported, letters filed—it is ready to be evaluated by the admissions committee. But what *is* an admissions committee? Who actually sits on this committee? Admissions committees at business schools come in many different sizes and flavors. Smaller regional programs may not have a committee at all. Some schools have committees of two or three, some as many as ten. Business schools commonly have an advisory committee on admissions, which advises the director of admissions and his or her officers (assistant deans and directors). In addition to these officers, the committee usually includes faculty members, administrators, students, alumni, and even psychologists. The committee sometimes acts only as an advisor on matters of admission policy, rather than in an operational capacity. More commonly, though, the committee is one that is largely advisory but also helps the admissions officers decide difficult or borderline cases. At many schools, all decisions concerning applicants are actually made by the committee as a group.

As far as the individuals on the committee go, they'll represent the widest range of personality and diversity of experience. The elements they have in common are a high degree of intelligence, a strong personal opinion and personality, an uncanny ability to accurately gauge the potential of an applicant, an ability to articulate clearly and listen closely, and a deep commitment and dedication to admitting the very best qualified applicants. Each member will have his or her own input and influence upon the composition of the entering class, reflecting each's distinctly different personality and viewpoint. Because most committee members will have been a part of the school in one capacity or another for some time, they'll be in a good position to determine whether the applicant will be an addition to the school's classroom and social environment.

All committee members share the common goal of admitting students who fit the espoused profile. This profile is usually one that calls for mature, motivated, focused, intelligent, well-rounded, competent, career-oriented, unique, interesting, and fun men and women. The only way to successfully achieve this goal is to be a person possessing some or all of these qualities. That is, "it takes one to know one."

Finally, committee members want to see you succeed in attaining your educational and career goals. Be assured that your application will be given a fair reading, and in most cases you'll be given any benefit of doubt. Because committee members are positive in their outlook, your overall approach to the application process should be positive as well.

How Will They Decide Your Case?

Highly selective business schools have seen their applicant pools grow despite the declining marketplace conditions. Larger applicant pools, combined with efforts to achieve greater diversity in entering classes, have made the admissions process seem more mysterious than ever to prospective MBAs. To add to this mystery, the selection process is more subjective now than ever before. What is it that goes on behind closed doors, during those long months between the time you send in your application and your notification of acceptance or rejection? How is it that an entering class is selected, anyway? What factors make a difference when the decisions are being fine-tuned by the committee?

As previously discussed, selection committees are quite varied in composition and number. But no matter the size and shape, there are two basic approaches that will be used in deciding your case. The first is a "blind read," whereby two committee members are given the same application to evaluate. Neither is aware of the other's comments or evaluation until after the fact. If the two readers agree in their evaluation, the decision is made. If they disagree, it is possible that a single, third reader will break the tie. At this point, though, rather than having only one more reader evaluate the file, the application may undergo the second basic approach—a group discussion. Members of the committee are given copies of the application, discussion takes place, and a joint decision is made. This is more time consuming and is more frequently used with candidates who have marginal or borderline qualifications. Let's take a look at how these processes work at one representative, selective business school.

The application has been completed. It is then read by an admissions officer responsible for the geographic area of the application's origin. The applicant is evaluated both objectively and subjectively. The objective appraisal is based on number of years of work experience, undergraduate school and grades, GMAT scores, and academic letters of reference. The subjective evaluation is more subtle and concerns itself with who the applicant is as a person as evinced by what he or she discloses in the personal essays. Once the applicant has been rated in these ways, the candidate's credentials are summarized in a written synopsis. If the applicant falls into one extreme or the other—positively, absolutely accept or positively, absolutely reject—then the officer makes that recommendation, with the file to be reviewed for final decision by the director. The rest of the files (the vast majority) are then given to a second reader, usually another admissions officer or faculty member, who follows the same procedure. The two-person blind read process results in three groups of applicants: those to whom the school will extend an offer of admission, those who don't qualify for admission, and those composing the middle ground: solid prospective MBAs who can all handle the rigors of the curriculum. These files go to committee.

Again, all committees have the same function: to make the tough choices between many equally qualified and able candidates. Applicants are presented, recommendations are given by previous reviewers, discussion and debate are undertaken, and finally a joint decision is reached. At this point, the committee does its best to admit prospective MBAs on the basis of what sets them apart and on their potential contribution to the classroom and campus. This is the most difficult task to undertake, especially when thousands of applicants are well qualified. Committees spend long hours hard at work at the difficult selection process. The decisions are entirely subjective at this point. Committees like to think their decisions are fair, at least to them. But be aware that although decisions are based in part on objective criteria, they are in the final analysis personal judgments of a number of factors. This subjectivity is what accounts for the same applicant being accepted to Harvard but being rejected by Wharton. Different *people* are making the decisions.

To better understand the process, consider that admissions officers of selective business schools must face many pressure-packed issues. They have the responsibility of implementing the school's overall admissions policy, but the individual decisions are left to the judgment of the committee members actually reading the files. The school's president often articulates the overall mission of the program in the school's brochure so that prospective MBAs can better understand the kinds of students who might best profit from the experience. Highly selective business schools have great interest in enrolling a first-year class with a broad base of work experience as well as ethnic, geographic, and personal diversity. You'll rarely find these policies quantified, but admissions directors know all the groups that need to be represented by the entering class. When fall arrives, the committee and school can only hope for an academically and intellectually exciting class of prospective MBAs who not only will contribute to campus life for two years, but who also will graduate and go on to make significant contributions to business and society at large. Making judgments about applicants that will bring about these kinds of achievements is no easy job.

Conclusion

It may at this point be redundant, and certainly obvious: Selective business schools deny admission to students who are as well qualified as those they admit. The decision to accept or reject is based on the personal and quite subjective views of the individuals reading your application. It is impossible to predict who will read your application; however, as we'll cover in subsequent chapters, there are very definite strategies for battling and offsetting the subjective nature of the MBA admissions process.

5

The Competitive Candidate

In this chapter, we'll briefly discuss the nature of the competitive candidate, and what it takes to get into the better business schools in the nation. It is important for the reader to understand that there is no such creature as the "ideal" or "perfect" applicant, and attempting to measure one's own qualifications against such a fictional person can only lead to discouragement. Focus on those characteristics that match up positively with your own personality, and success will be just around the corner.

What Are Admissions Committees Looking for?

Admissions officers love to answer, "I don't exactly know, but I'll know it when I see it." This is an honest answer, but not too helpful. Generally, they look for intellectual ability, demonstrated management ability and potential for future growth, and outstanding personal characteristics. Specifically, this means top grades and test scores, extensive and varied work experience, and traits such as maturity, motivation, leadership, thoughtfulness, competitiveness, aggressiveness, self-awareness, ethical standards, responsibility, management potential, and personal integrity.

Responsible decision making and integrity are becoming increasingly important at the top schools. These rather intangible qualities are assessed through the many personal essays you'll write. Even more specifically, they'll look to see if you have a well-thought-out career plan, that you understand the strategic importance and timing of your MBA in relation to your past decisions, and that you know how it will fit into your future plans. They want to admit focused, intent individuals who know who they are, why they've taken the direction they have so far, why the MBA is important *now* (as opposed to, say, next year), and how they will apply what they learn in the MBA program. Because there are always many more outstanding applicants than there are places in the classes of selective schools, admissions committees, then, seek compelling reasons to admit candidates, rather than finding excuses to reject them.

A common misconception among prospective MBAs is that magic, predetermined formulas exist for admission to the top schools. Not true. Candidates are not categorized to any great extent and are not expected to fit into any such mold. Admissions committees seek to admit individuals who will challenge their faculty and provide synergy in the student-faculty interaction as well as in the student-student interaction. They seek diversity among students, as this is a critical ingredient in the makeup of each MBA class. Students who will be admitted come from a wide variety of educational, experiential, and cultural backgrounds.

Conclusion

Consider yourself a competitive candidate, as every prospective MBA has the potential to gain acceptance to the school of his or her choice. In the remainder of this book, thoughts and strategies for meeting these competitive criteria will be offered and explained in a practical and effective way.

6

What Makes a Successful Application?

In this chapter, the various factors going into the admissions decision will be examined in relation to their relative importance to the overall process of selection. The various elements of any application may be properly categorized as either objective criteria or subjective criteria. Objective factors include work experience, extracurricular activities, letters of recommendation, undergraduate grades, and GMAT scores. Likened to the sport of gymnastics, these objective factors can be thought of as the "compulsories." Subjective factors, which carry greater relative importance than objective criteria, include essays and, increasingly, interviews.

OBJECTIVE CRITERIA

How Much Work Experience Is Needed?

The short answer to this question is not less than three years in order to be a competitive applicant to the highly selective schools. The average number of years of post-college experience at the top schools is more like four or five years. In order to be competitive, then, you should wait until you have at least three years of work experience behind you. Years ago, top schools accepted a large percentage of applicants directly out of undergraduate college. Now, most schools accept only one to two percent of their applicant pool having no work experience; these individuals are brilliant young women and men who have made outstanding achievements in college and community activities as well as summer jobs.

The reasons for the great emphasis placed on full-time postcollege work experience are well-founded. First, the more selective schools seek to admit mature individuals who have been out in the work force long enough to have developed a long-range career plan. These individuals are better able to realize the value of the MBA. The career focus of a person with several years of professional experience is much greater than that of one with only one or two years' experience. And since the leading business schools seek to admit those who know why they want and need an MBA, it makes sense to admit applicants who possess this work experience. Second, the curricula at the top schools require a wide range of student skills and experience in order to be most effective. Functional job experience is a necessity to acquire a degree of familiarity with approaches to working with and through other people to accomplish tasks. Third, in the view of admissions committees, full-time experience in business, government, military service, or community work exposes individuals to management, permits development of an understanding of the complexity of human organizations, and provides opportunities to assume responsibility and take initiative in solving organizational, technical, and analytical problems.

Additionally, work experience enhances one's ability to contribute to the educational process of an MBA program and to arrive at a more realistic understanding of the relevance of the curriculum to personal goals and interests. You should be in no great hurry to get your MBA. Wait until you're in the competitive age and experience range (27 years old, five years experience) before you apply. Of course, applying to less selective schools is always an option, but the rewards of waiting to apply to the top schools will be well worth it in the long run.

What Kinds of Experience Are Best?

Business. Government. Military service. Community office. As long as it is full-time and postcollege, it's good experience. You'll note by glancing through the applications of business schools that work experience involving leadership, responsibility, and managerial problem-solving challenges are emphasized. The jobs you seek should have these qualities to them. It is not so important what your job title is; most applicants, though, overemphasize the importance of title. Every admissions officer will assert that the lessons learned and diversity of experience gained through a job are much more valuable than the name of the position itself. It matters not to the committee whether you've managed a Wendy's or worked for Goldman Sachs on Wall Street. What *does* matter is your reason(s) for taking the job in the first place, how you saw this job fitting into your career development, what experiences you gained, and how these experiences contributed to your decision to seek an MBA at this time. You must be able to talk about personal and professional achievements on the job. You must be able to discuss leadership roles you assumed on the job. You must be able to relate to the committee positions of responsibility you held on the job. Finally, you must be able to convince them that these positions have allowed you to realize your need to obtain an MBA.

If your present job is lacking in these areas, you should hold off applying until such time as you've gained these types of experience. Actively seek leadership roles, both inside and outside work. Don't worry that you haven't attained a job title that sounds impressive. The most impressive-sounding titles are often deficient for purposes of business school applications. Concentrate on extracting as much knowledge, responsibility, and diversity of experience as you can before applying to the selective business schools.

How Important Are Undergraduate Grades?

The importance of your college academic record is inversely related to the number of years of work experience you have under your belt. In other words, if you've been working for 10 years, the importance of your college grade point average as an indicator of your present intellectual ability is greatly diminished. Your analytical prowess will be judged more on the basis of your work experience. If, on the other hand, you're a college senior attempting to gain admission to a selective school, your grades will figure heavily in the objective evaluation of your file, since you have nothing else upon which the committee can gauge your intellectual powers (excepting your GMAT scores).

Grades can simply be thought of as one of four or five components in your statistical package. The discussion of undergraduate grades is, however, and pardon the pun, academic. There is nothing you can do at this point to change them. And while the average GPA hovers around 3.4 (on a 4.0 scale), it is not the case that a "weeding out" process or indexing of applications on the basis of grades occurs, as is the case in law schools. Remember, though, that successful applicants will naturally have the aptitude to complete graduate academic study. In short, don't let the fear that your grades aren't good enough keep you from applying to a top MBA school. There are many (and more important) factors that go into the admissions decisions of the better business schools. If you are truly worried about your grades, enroll in a few graduate-level courses to demonstrate your present capacity to perform at the graduate level.

How Important Are GMAT Scores?

Harvard has a great answer to this question: "Not at all!" (As an aside, please note that not only does Harvard not require GMAT scores, but they don't accept them at all—if you send them GMAT scores, it may work to your disadvantage.) While it is probably unlikely that other top schools will follow Harvard's lead in eliminating GMAT scores, it is certainly somewhat indicative of the relative importance of the test scores at the better schools. Again, average scores are high at around 630, but it's more a case of admitting all-around excellent candidates than of selection on the basis of test scores.

It's safe to say that the top schools rely on GMAT scores to act as "equalizers" of undergraduate academic records, that is, as a uniform standard against which everyone's performance can be somewhat reliably measured. This is important to the admissions office, since undergraduate curriculum and majors often differ in rigor and grading. GMAT scores are like grades in that you should never not apply because your scores fall below the average scores at your desired schools. Remember that no minimums are set for GPAs and GMATs at most schools. And again, other factors will easily make up for seemingly poor scores. GMAT scores do differ from grades in one important aspect—your GMAT score is within your control to some degree. If you prepare properly, GMAT scores should not even be an issue. Everyone is capable of scoring competitively on the test if they spend the time to prepare. Chapter 9 will discuss the GMAT in detail.

How Important Are Extracurricular Activities?

Important! Organized extracurricular activities provide an excellent opportunity to display leadership and managerial potential and willingness to participate in group endeavors. The better business schools are looking for potential leaders, and if you haven't gotten involved and demonstrated leadership, your chances of being a future business leader will seem gloomy. If your lack of college activity was due to a heavy courseload, you should make sure you have an outstanding record of leadership in work-related activities. If you lack relevant work experience, extracurricular activities become increasingly important as an indication of your organizational and leadership potential. The MBA is not the right degree for the quiet scholar.

Hobbies and avocations are equally important, because they'll provide the committee with a good look at your life away from your job. In all cases, it's not the number of activities that's important, it's the quality and nature of those experiences. You must be able to show a well-roundedness—the selection folks are interested to see if you'll fit in socially and outside the classroom.

How Important Are Letters of Reference?

Admissions committees place a good deal of importance on letters of recommendation, because they act to verify that you're as great and wonderful as you claim you are. They are an essential ingredient in a successful application, and acceptees all will have had excellent references. Your chances of getting in with mediocre or poor references are decreased, because you'll be unable to justify the reasons for them.

All of these—work experience, grades, GMAT scores, activities, and letters of reference—are part of the objective criteria. You must have this package, because all successful applicants have relatively equal objective packages behind them. All of these elements have the potential, when negative, to decrease or deny your admission chances to a top program, yet no single positive factor will really enable automatic acceptance. The subjective criteria that we'll discuss next, however, have the potential to override all objective criteria and enable your admission to be realized.

SUBJECTIVE CRITERIA

How Important Are the Personal Essays?

In a nutshell, VITAL and ALL-IMPORTANT! At the top-ranked MBA programs, the answers you provide in the many and varied essays can make or break your chances of admission. Consider the fact that admissions committees at these schools receive thousands of applications, the vast majority of which reveal superior and relatively equal objective packages: good grades and scores, excellent letters of reference, important outside activities, and relevant work experience. But what about the person behind the statistics? How can the committee differentiate between these thousands of qualified applicants? You guessed it—the essays.

The essay is not only the major factor in successful admissions, it is the only factor that is in *your total control*. The essays have a dual function: They not only help the admissions committee decide whom to accept or reject, but also allow you the opportunity to argue your case for admission. Essays are probably the one sure shot you'll have at convincing the committee that they need you. As we'll see in the next chapter, the process of writing essays is the most difficult part of applying to business school, but the most important part. They'll provide the all-important "sparkle" to your file. Without this sparkle, your application will meld into a frighteningly similar collection of other applications.

These are *personal* essays—so you must make them personal. Committees don't look for the "right" or necessarily the most clever answer to a question. If you are sincere, write well, and are able to follow the guidelines described in Chapter 7, you'll be successful. Too many applicants make their applications look like embellished résumés. They cover up what the committee wants to see: the qualities that set them apart from the others.

How Important Are Interviews?

Two years ago, interviews played only a minor role in the admissions processes of one or two schools. Five years ago, they were practically nonexistent. The trend now, it seems, is to place a greater emphasis on an evaluative interview at schools such as Wharton, Tuck, Kellogg and Cornell. Others now actively interview borderline or wait-listed applicants. If the schools to which you apply request that you attend a personal interview, it's an indication that some importance is placed on a face-to-face meeting. It's a bit too soon to tell exactly how the interview figures into the process; however, given that interviews are extensions of the personal essays and subjective criteria, it's safe to say that a successful interview can sway a committee in your favor, especially if you're a borderline applicant.

To take an example, in the recent admission year, Wharton interviewed over 2,000 of their applicant pool. This represented a third of all applicants and was an increase of nearly 25 percent over the previous year, and more than eight times the number interviewed five years ago. They expect to interview the majority of their applicant pool this year. If nothing else, evaluative interviews allow the admissions committee to assess the qualitative abilities and interpersonal skills of applicants, in addition to reviewing written records and quantitative measures. Wharton claims that the true potential of its incoming class was measured in these face-to-face meetings. The interviews helped identify and bring a diverse and motivated group of students to the school.

Applications That Committees Dread

The following types of applications usually are tossed into the "circular file" as the committee members roll their eyes and say, "Give me a break!"

The "Lead Balloon"

These applicants take themselves much too seriously. They've called on the forces of the galaxy to support them. Letters of reference numbering in the teens, by everyone from the President to the Pope, accompany the application. Lists of activities, awards, jobs, and hobbies go on for pages, approaching a Michener novel in length. The essays are ponderous, boring, overedited, and "beige."

The "Helium Balloon"

These applicants obviously filled out their applications in front of the TV, between commercials. They use one school's application essays to apply to another school, thinking they've outsmarted the admissions committee. They hardly had time to type out their answers. Mistakes and omissions pepper the application. The tone is flippant and nonchalant.

The "Radical"

These prospective MBAs, in an effort to be different and unique, come off as eccentric and not at all in the image of the school. Essays are written in crayon, and are in rhyming verse. They've spent two years in a nudist colony "finding themselves" and are now sure the MBA is right for them.

The "Hype"

These prospective MBAs have presented a full-blown advertising glitz that would make Ogilvy blush. They include 8×10 glossies with video résumés. Essays are written in an insincere, albeit flashy style.

A Few Things to Consider Before You Begin

1. *Organize.* Make folders for each school to which you're applying, label them carefully, and keep any and all materials concerning a particular school in that folder. This will greatly facilitate the process (see Appendix A.)

2. *Photocopy Everything.* Never, ever work from the original application. Work from copies until you've

worked all the kinks out of your application, then recopy the information onto the original.

3. *Devise a Schedule and Stick to it.* This is the only way you'll give your applications and essays proper attention and thought. Keep track of your progress as you go. Set dates for letters of reference to be received, transcripts to be sent for, and GMAT scores to be received.

4. *Be Realistic.* Avoid the all-too-common mistake of tying all your hopes to one school or one group of schools, and of creating the "perfect" (yet completely mythical) place. In addition to the highly selective schools, apply to a couple that are less in the limelight than the top programs. This will act as a backup, "just in case...."

Conclusion

Admission at the top-ranked business schools is a highly competitive and subjective process, more so than with any other type of graduate program. The more prestigious the school, the tougher the competition will be. You've got about a 15 to 20 percent chance of acceptance at the top schools. The next section of the book will show you how to tip those odds in your favor. It *can* be done!

PART THREE

■

THE STRATEGY—BEATING THE COMPETITION

Part III at a Glance

This section forms the heart of the book. Read it carefully, then reread it—twice. The chapters are arranged in order of decreasing importance, so that Chapter 7 is the most important, while Chapter 11 is the least important. Chapter 7 discusses in great detail how to write the crucial essays required for admission to the better business schools. Chapter 8 covers letters of reference, from how to choose recommenders to finalizing the letters. Chapter 9 provides a brief synopsis of the Graduate Management Admissions Test and gives tips from an experienced test taker's point of view. Chapter 10 details the interview process in its current status, and Chapter 11 concludes the book.

7

The Essays—How to Present Yourself

As discussed in the previous chapter, the essays are an all-important component of the application to a selective business school. It is the one factor that can totally make or break your admissions chances. It is imperative that this chapter be read in great detail and suggestions closely followed. This part of the application process is the most difficult and time-consuming. It is suggested that between 30 and 40 hours be spent writing each application's essays. This chapter will give step-by-step writing strategies as well as give a close look at specific essay questions.

What Does the Committee Want to Hear?

Wrong approach! This is the most frequently asked question, and it is the absolute worst way to plan a writing strategy. Ask any admissions officer about the most important characteristic in an essay, and they'll respond across the board with, "Honesty." Why? Easy! Admissions committees, above all, want to know about *you* and your personality in order to get to know you. Much time and money is spent designing essays that "flesh out" an applicant's personal side. Writing essays in an attempt to "give the committee what they want to hear" is not an honest approach and will sound artificial and generic. Questions such as, "Should I tell them I like new wave music?" or "Should I say I'm a Democrat or a Republican?" or "Should I say I want to major in finance or marketing?" are completely ridiculous from the standpoint of how to present yourself. Every prospective MBA dreams of the magic essay that will get him or her in automatically. Unfortunately, there's no magic formula. Many admissions officers will tell you that they don't know what they want, but they know it when they see it. There are, however, certain characteristics that must be present. Let's discuss those characteristics.

What You Must Convey About Yourself and How to Say It

First of all, think about the essays as an integral component of the application. Why are they there in the first place? Upon reading the catalogs of the various top business schools in the country, you'll note that each school, virtually without exception, states that they seek to admit motivated, mature, unique, intelligent, and career-minded *individuals*. This, then, is the reason for so many specific essays. In order to find these individuals, dozens of difficult and distinctly different essay questions are asked of potential MBAs. Remember, chances are you'll never meet with the admissions committee in person. The essays must go in your stead and present the complete picture of you. Each essay requires an honest, thoughtful, and insightful answer. Honesty is a virtue in any essay, as it is in work and life. This quality, above all, must characterize each of your essays.

Your goal in writing the essays, of course, is to *get in*. Thus the problem becomes a marketing dilemma. Briefly, you must present a persuasive, forceful, logical, honest, unique, interesting, and insightful *argument* for your admission into the school. If the admissions committee walks away with anything less of a response to your essays than, "We *must* have this person in our program," you have failed to solve the marketing problem, and your chances of being accepted are slim. Further, you must present yourself as a distinctly unique person with something attractive and fresh to add to the school and to the classroom. You must convey how you see yourself fitting into the professional world. Most importantly, you must come across as a motivated and mature individual who knows why the MBA is the right choice at this particular time, how your past has led you to this point and prepared you to make this decision, and how the MBA fits into your career plan—which necessitates your having a career plan!

Almost every admissions director will say that the school seeks to accept an individual who is clear and forceful in articulating why he or she wishes to pursue the MBA and why the MBA is a necessary and strategic career move. You must have a good degree of focus about your future and be able to articulate that in your essays. Woven into the argument for why you must obtain your MBA will be your past experiences, both professional and educational. A committee member must be able to read your essays and think, "Yes, it certainly makes sense for Bob to get his MBA at this time; I can certainly see how his decision has evolved and come to fruition, based on his experiences. I think his ideas for his career in banking are sound as well." The undercurrent which must flow through each and every essay, no matter what the topic, must be one of, "Why the MBA? Why now? How does it fit in?" At this point, you may be wondering to yourself why this is so crucial to an admissions committee. Remember, the stated goal of these programs is to train managers and business leaders. If you cannot present what is in essence a business plan for your career, certainly one must question your ability to submit a business report or plan in the professional arena. Admissions committees expect you to take the same kind of care with your presentation and content as you would in a management position. So, start now to think through why you are seeking an MBA, and begin to formulate a business plan for your career—a career which necessitates the MBA. Again, you must be honest, thoughtful and insightful, but don't mistake this advice to mean that the only applicants who succeed in gaining admission to a good school are those who have very *precise* ideas of what they want to do with the rest of their lives. In fact, many prospective MBAs are in a period of transition in their lives. You may be reevaluating your career, hoping to change directions, but unsure exactly which direction to take. If that's the case, be honest. Say so!

Changing careers is actually a good reason to pursue an MBA. The point is, it is much better to be honest about your future than falsely precise. On the other hand, vagueness is not a virtue, so to say that most successful applicants write essays revealing a strong sense of purpose is true. Since the medium in which you must convey all of these qualities is the written word, you must take care to write extremely well. How else will you be able to present yourself accurately? The form your essays take can be very important. How you communicate using the English language is important—the ability to articulate your thoughts in a clear and concise fashion is a must. Admissions committees tend to be sensitive to poor writing skills, because although they aren't necessarily looking for future authors or scholars, they want literate future business leaders. There's no question that writing style makes a difference. Good writers are convincing and engaging. Ideas flow smoothly, making the reader's job much easier and more enjoyable. To make this writing task even more difficult, you must be specific in your approach and answer, while also being intriguing. This doesn't mean that you must know in which position and company you will work, but it does mean having specifics to support your answers. You must be able to organize your thoughts well because you'll be faced with length limitations. Further, you must take care that your essays look neat. If you've taken the proper care to be neat and careful, it will lend a bit of professionalism to the presentation. To reiterate and enumerate the general qualities of successful essays:

1. Clarity of Purpose
A sense of direction must prevail. Do you know why you wish to obtain your MBA? Have you thoroughly

thought through your career path? Do you know what you wish to get out of an MBA program, what skills you wish to develop in the process, and how you envision using your education in the future? Have you presented everything in an honest, thoughtful, unique, and insightful way? Have you been appropriately specific in stating your purpose?

2. Clarity of Expression
Have you carefully articulated your response? Have you avoided reiterating information contained in other parts of the application? Have you made your points in a concise way, supporting your assertions with specific facts about you, your background, and your personality? Are your essays well-written, detailed, and responsive to the question? Have you neither overelaborated nor understated? Have you avoided a monotonous tone and style? Have you avoided using too many big words and amorphous adjectives and not enough colorful details and observations? Have you adhered to word limitations?

3. Uniqueness of Expression
Have you presented yourself as an interesting individual? Have you shed new light on an old subject, given a fresh slant to a common notion? Have you locked onto a "hook"—an angle that will set you apart from the rest of the crowd? Will an admissions officer remember you? Have you avoided a dry, overedited essay that will put the reader to sleep? Have you conveyed your personality effectively to the committee through your essay answers? Have you shown different facets of your personality, without

being outrageous? Have you been entertaining without being gimmicky? Have you captivated your reader? Have you said what you feel? Have you been careful to back up wit and humor with meaningful points? Does your expressed uniqueness mesh with the rest of the application? Have you kept in mind that an actual person will be reading your essays?

4. Forcefulness of Expression
Have you presented a persuasive collection of essays that will successfully "sell" *you* to the committee? Have you marketed yourself as an invaluable addition to the program? Have you avoided being unduly modest? Have you properly "tooted your own horn"? Have you been justifiably proud of your achievements? Have you *said something?*

5. Honesty of Expression
Have you given the committee "you, the whole you, and nothing but you"? Have you been frank about your strengths and weaknesses? Does the reader get a real sense of your world view and personality? Honest essays are the best essays to read, and the easiest to write. Concocting ridiculous anecdotes, attention-getting schemes, or a fictitious portrait is a big waste of time and energy. You must be vibrant, but not gimmicky. You must be businesslike in your approach, but don't feed the committee dull, pompous lines.

It is imperative that each of your essays contain these five qualities. We will see how all of these factors are to be applied when the individual essay question types are addressed later in the chapter.

Essay Writing Strategy and the Writing Process

One of the hardest things for any writer to do is to begin putting ideas down on paper. In the next few pages, strategies for getting started will be discussed and a step-by-step plan for beginning the essays reviewed. Assuming that you have not written any autobiographical or personal statements about yourself since high school, this process can be alien and frustrating. One of the most important things to remember throughout is to relax. Have fun with the essays! If you do, it'll show in your responses, and the admissions officers reading your essays will pick up on your enthusiasm.

▤ WRITING STRATEGY #1
Start Early!

Successful essays take much time, thought, and rewriting. Do not wait until a month before the application is due, because by that time it will be too late. Pick a target completion date somewhere around four months before the application deadline. Begin at least three months in advance of this target date, and plan to spend at least 30 writing hours on your first application. Remember, you'll be starting from scratch on the first application. Get all of the applications to all of the schools to which you'll be applying together, and read the essay questions. Read them every day after that, so that they remain constantly in the back of your mind. You'll subconsciously begin to formulate general responses in your head. This is the optimal situation to be in three months before the target completion date and will prime you for the next step.

WRITING STRATEGY #2
Review Your Life, Experiences, and Goals

This is tougher to do than it sounds. It is very difficult to think about and remember experiences, accomplishments, and other relevant facts. You can make yourself more aware of your experiences and goals by brainstorming. This is an important strategy, because it makes you think in specifics and is an important part of the writing preparatory phase. The best way to engage in this strategy is to pick up paper and pen and begin to make lists, and ask and answer some important questions about yourself.

A. Make a Few Lists

To get the memory working, make lists of all of the following:

Honors, awards, or distinctions
Extracurricular activities
Community and professional activities
Leadership positions
Hobbies and avocations
All paid positions you've held full-time
Accomplishments in those jobs
Publications, research papers, etc.
Career goals
Things that make you happy

Don't leave anything out, and take about three weeks to complete the lists. You'll begin to remember more and more things as you go. Your goal here is just to put down on paper as much as you can remember, no matter how important or relevant you think it is. (See Appendix D, Personal Data File.)

B. Think: What Kind of Person Am I?
Use simple adjectives here—nothing complicated, just *get it down!* Be as specific as you can; ask friends to help you. Remember, you're brainstorming here. Descriptions such as "motivated," "career-minded," "competitive," "analytical," and "ambitious" tell much about you as a person. Pick the top five or so qualities you think best define you.

C. Think: What Evidence Shows That I'm This Type of Person?
Now relate the lists you made in Section A to the adjectives in Section B. Find events or experiences in your life in which these qualities are best shown. You may even write a paragraph about it. Your goal here is to substantiate your assertions about yourself. At the very least, match up on paper the five qualities which describe you with two or three experiences or achievements for each quality listed.

D. Think: What Do I Want to Do With My Life?
Write short answers to all of the following questions:
What kind of position do you want out of business school?
What about five years after graduation? Ten years?
What kind of person would you like to be then?

What is the relationship between the MBA and your career goals?
How will the MBA help you attain your goals?
What is your vision of yourself in the future?

This will take some time, but it is time well spent. The answers to these questions will form the heart of most of your essay answers and will provide an excellent analysis of yourself.

E. Think: What Have I Done With My Life?

Think about your past and where you've come from to reach this point in your life. Write short answers to all of the following questions:

Why did you go to college?
Why did you study what you did?
Why did you pick the jobs you've accepted to this point?
Have you changed your goals? Your interests?
What has led you to the pursuit of the MBA?

Thinking about your past is important, as it gives you a view of the stages you've gone through and decisions you've made that have led you to determine that the MBA is right for you.

F. Link Your Past, Present, and Future

Now relate the answers in Section D to the answers in Section E. Note how the past has shaped your future.

≡ WRITING STRATEGY #3
Make an Outline

This is a mandatory step in any writing and is most critical for your admissions essays. With a good outline to follow, writing the essay itself is fairly easy, because you'll already have done the hard part: the thinking. Outlines ensure that all of your ideas are included and that they are presented in logical sequence, making your essay flow smoothly from idea to idea. An outline provides organization—an introduction, body, and conclusion that are well-planned and well-developed.

As a practical matter, you should write an outline for each different type of essay you'll be facing. If two essay questions are very similar, you needn't write two entirely different outlines. Many people like to begin with the application to Harvard Business School, even if they aren't applying to the school. There are some 12 essays to write. Almost every base is covered, and strict word limits exist. It is by far the most comprehensive of the applications, and outlining answers to each question on the application will mostly complete your thinking and outlining. A generic outline might look like this:

I. Introduction
- A general statement, a main idea or thesis, and an eyecatcher

II. Body
- Answer the question, using specific examples and details
- Answer hidden, unwritten questions

III. Conclusion
- Personalize your essay
- Summarize your thoughts; relate your answer to the question, "Why the MBA?"

WRITING STRATEGY #4
Write a Rough Draft

You should count on writing at least three drafts of each essay. Anything short of three times is still rough and not truly competitive. Successful applicants write and rewrite many times before being satisfied with a final draft. As a first step, though, you must get a draft on paper. Use your outline, adhere to word limits, and adjust your answer to the reader.

Constructing a great introduction is crucial. Remember that admissions officers read thousands of answers to the same essay topic. The introduction is a very influential part of the essay and one of the hardest to write. A powerful introduction will wake the reader up, and chances are then very good that the rest of your essay will be read with interest and attentiveness. A poor introduction tells the reader that she or he is about to read another one of thousands of similar, "ho-hum" essays.

The body of the essay should directly address the question asked, focusing on the aspects of your life that specifically support your answer. The ideas must be developed fully. The conclusion will then logically flow from the body of the argument. You must always remember to interpret the parts of your life that you are relating to the reader: What did you learn from a certain experience, and how did it contribute to your desire to get an MBA? The conclusion, like the introduction, must give the reader a favorable impression of you. Remember, personalize the essay, and end on an upbeat note!

Adjusting the essay to the reader is an important aspect of writing an appropriate answer. You can safely assume that your reader will be intelligent and eclectic in background: Don't talk down to your reader. Remember that your reader will determine your acceptance or rejection. Be assertive without being cheeky and disrespectful. You can assume that your audience is sympathetic to you, but don't depend on that sympathy to get you an indulgent reading. Don't assume that your readers are so sympathetic that you need not persuade them of your excellence. If you ever find yourself saying, "They'll know what I mean," you're in trouble. Clear, well-developed ideas gain reader sympathy.

≡ WRITING STRATEGY #5
Proofread, Edit, and Rewrite

If you scrimp on this step, all of your effort will be for naught. The essential ingredient of the successful essay is time: time to think and rethink, time to write and rewrite, time to read and reread, time to proofread and reproofread, time to edit and redit. Never read and rewrite an essay on the same day. Give it time! When you return to your essays, you will see them in a fresh light. There are two levels at which you must go over your essays: content and mechanics.

First, read your essays for content. Are you satisfied with what you've said? Do they meet the five criteria of a good essay? Have you conveyed the image you wish to project? Should certain ideas be expanded? Should others be deleted? Make good and wise use of your red pen—be as objective as you can. Put yourself in the reader's place. Do you walk away saying, "Wow! We need this person in our classroom!"?

Second, check for mechanics. Check spelling, grammar, usage, and punctuation. Use a dictionary and thesaurus. Take care that your essays are as mechnically tight as they possibly can be.

Rewrite your essays, making the corrections, additions, and deletions to content and mechanics. Let the essays sit on your desk for a week or so, then go back to them. Chances are, you'll have thought of yet other changes you wish to make. Take care, however, not to edit out the "flavor" of your essays. This is a fine line to walk, so be careful. Overediting and underediting are both shortcomings to a successful essay. If you've followed these strategies and kept in mind the five criteria to a good essay, you'll have a successful application in your hands. Let's now take a look at how specifically to address the various questions on business school applications.

How to Address the Different Types of Essay Questions

There are 10 basic categories of essay questions that you'll be faced with. Of course, not every application has each type of question, but all applications will have at least three of the following types of essays: "You, the MBA, and Your Career," "Substantial Achievements or Accomplishments," "Leadership and Responsibility," "Self-Analysis," "Ethical Dilemmas," "For Fun," "Painful or Difficult Experiences," "Creative Brainbenders," "Academics," and the "Optional" Essay. In the following pages, each type of essay will be discussed in detail, with actual and successful essays given as examples; analyses of sample essays will follow.

"You, the MBA, and Your Career"

This is perhaps the most important essay you will write. Every business school application will have an essay that falls into this category, and most schools place it as the first essay to write. Note below some of the different ways the same question is asked by various schools:

> *What factors led you to decide that graduate education at Harvard Business School would be helpful to your career plan? (Harvard)*
>
> *Clearly and specifically identify your post-MBA short-term and long-term career objectives. Discuss three experiences which have most significantly affected the development of these goals. (Wharton)*
>
> *Tell us about those influences that have significantly shaped who you are today. How do you see your career developing? How will an MBA further that development? Why are you applying to Stanford? (Stanford)*
>
> *Why have you decided to enter an MBA program? Why have you decided to apply to UCLA in particular? What other options for next year, aside from remaining in your current position, have you seriously considered? (UCLA)*
>
> *What are your academic goals, and why is the University of Chicago's MBA program particularly suited to help you attain them? How does your intended course of study relate to your career choice and professional objectives? (Chicago)*

The Essays—How to Present Yourself   59

Discuss your intended career path and what you see as Kellogg's place in that path. (Kellogg)

Over the past decade, a world economy has clearly emerged, replacing isolated national economies. Discuss the effect that internationalization may have on your future responsibilities as a manager, both generally and as regards your chosen field, and what you hope to learn at MIT to enable you to meet this challenge. (Sloan)

It should now be abundantly clear why the first criterion discussed in the opening pages of this chapter is so important. To reiterate, it is essential that you are clear as to your purpose in getting an MBA at the particular school to which you are applying, clear on your career aspirations, and clear as to what led you to decide to pursue the MBA. You *must* have a business plan for your career. Otherwise, you can't realistically know why you want to get your MBA, and you will be unable to articulate convincingly to the committee your need for an MBA. (Unfortunately, "in order to make more money" is an unacceptable answer, although very probably an honest one.) Let's take a look at some very well-written and successful responses to the Kellogg essay.

■ Response #1.

The English novelist Edward Bulwer once wrote that "The man who succeeds above his fellows is the one who, early in life, clearly discerns this object, and towards that object habitually directs his powers. Even genius itself is but fine observation strengthened by fixity of purpose. Every man who observes vigilantly and resolves steadfastly grows unconsciously onto genius." The success I have experienced throughout my life is a result of my "fixity of purpose." My accomplishments in college and in the business arena are a reflection of my potential for the future and a plan I established early in my adult life. The next step in this plan provides for the diversification of the skills I have developed over the last four years and an advanced degree in public management. Although my exact career aspirations are far from complete, I do have a blueprint for success directing me towards one final goal.

For as long as I can remember, I have always had a fascination with politics and more specifically, with the workings of the Federal government. This interest, until my final year in college, seemed always to be more of a hobby and I had little interest in entering politics or government work in general. However, what I found during my four years at Clemson University was that although I had a keen interest in business, my true aspirations were in the public sector. My contention has always been that the people who are truly successful in the public sector, whether elected officials or high-ranking staff members, are the professionals with diverse backgrounds and experience. To that end, I have spent the past four years as an associate in the municipal investment banking industry gaining experience and cultivating my understanding of the fiscal workings of the public sector. After graduating from Clemson University, I accepted a job in New York with E.F. Hutton because I desired to be on the cutting edge of the municipal industry. In December of 1987, I left E.F. Hutton to work for Ehrlich Bober & Company because I was given the opportunity to work as the assistant to the Managing Director of Investment Banking of the only national firm which specializes in municipal finance. During the past four years, my challenge has been to design financings that would enable municipalities and state governments to raise money in the private sector. This was of special significance because the number of municipalities coming to market during this period was the largest in history. However, I now realize that I have reached a point in my career where my current job responsibilities and long-term career plans are at a crossroads. I have decided to once again advance to a new challenge and that challenge means moving into the field that holds the most interest and future for me. It is my intention to enter the public sector and pursue a career in government.

This fact alone does not justify business school or the necessity to enter at this time. But it has long been my belief that the government and the manner in which it provides services should be run like a business within the obvious structure and benefit of the democratic process. In concert with this fact is the importance, now more than ever, of the relationship between the public sector and private industry. As all levels of government face budget deficits, the care of the aged, educational concerns, crime, etc., it has become a necessity for public sector leaders to approach these problems and their possible solutions as a business would and for the public and private sectors to work together toward a common end. It is my desire to not only be a part of this process but to be a pioneer in the public/private sector cooperative development.

The question before me now becomes, why a Masters in Management from Kellogg, and why now? The answers to these questions are obvious in my mind. For all practical purposes, my learning curve within my field is now flat. After four years and a number of exciting challenges and responsibilities, it is time to move on. To remain in municipal investment banking would provide me with the opportunity to undertake larger financings with more responsibility but the additional learning benefit they would offer and the opportunity to apply that learning to further my career goals would no longer exist. At Kellogg, I could enhance the analytical skills I possess, while diversifying my business knowledge and practical application. My personality and drive has always been proactive as opposed to reactive. The curriculum, professors, students and most of all the administration at Kellogg lead me to believe that of all the national programs, Northwestern's would be best able to provide me with a complement to the skills I have and broaden my perspective for the future. As for the necessity of a Masters at this time, there is no doubt I could enter government and the political arena without it but I do not wish to just enter the arena, I intend to set precedents and establish policy. My experiences in the private sector have afforded me with a number of skills but in a very narrow area of the business world—investment banking. For me to truly succeed I must have the diversity of enhanced analytical and managerial skills which only a graduate degree in business can provide. Although public sector management has a long history in theory, its practical application began recently and is slow in developing. By working my way up in government I would only gain experience in government; that experience alone would not provide me with the tools or knowledge to effectively manage a governmental entity or coordinate a private company/public sector joint venture. Kellogg's core curriculum and institutional specialization in Public and Nonprofit Management would provide me with these tools at the right time in my career and enable me to succeed in public sector business.

I believe that over the next few years both politicians and the general public will realize that regardless of party affiliation and the rigid beliefs associated with them, state and local governments are facing a number of severe problems and the organization which can best solve those problems should and will be elected. I propose that private business initiatives in the public policy forum will provide many of these solutions. The time has now come for professional business expertise with real public sector experience and understanding. My long-term role within the public arena cannot be absolutely defined, but whether as a high-ranking staff member of the House Ways and Means Committee or a private consultant to the Office of Management and Budget, I plan to be a part of the public process. I feel that in the final analysis I have clearly discerned my object and will direct all my powers to that end. My strength as I look toward final success is a solid beginning and a fixed purpose.

■ Response #2

I wish to attend Kellogg because it will help me with my career plans to obtain a senior marketing position in a service company.

I have come to business indirectly. With an English and History degree from Stanford and varied extracurricular interests, I had always planned to enter journalism or magazine publishing. Through the Radcliffe Publishing Procedures Course, however, I landed in the publicity and promotion department at Putnam's Publishing.

After acquiring basic public relations training there, I ventured into more challenging p.r. territory at Fern Mallis Public Relations. In two very busy years, I handled full-time, multi-

pronged accounts for which I reported directly to the client. I also helped run the three-man office. I learned the intricacies of the interiors business and earned the respect of my clients.

I also won their business when Fern Mallis dismantled her company. With two of her former clients, I set up a new contract/home furnishings division at AC&R Public Relations. I was thrust into an active sales role and soon gained the firm additional new business. A subsequent promotion to Account Executive enabled me to interact with many departments on different accounts at this full-service advertising agency.

I was ready, after seven years in public relations, for a broader role in business planning and implementation. As marketing coordinator at PHH Neville Lewis, I have been directly responsible for new business, hence, the future of the firm. Along with the managing principal, I have set strategy and implemented programs to win new clients. It has been a challenging and rewarding stint.

I now want to accelerate my career in services marketing and, eventually, management. The Kellogg Masters of Management program will teach me the management concepts and tools that are a daily part of the business arena. Armed with a strong working knowledge of finance, operations, accounting and policy, I will be better prepared to analyze and solve the problems I will be facing as part of a decision-making team.

Having carefully researched graduate management programs, I feel that Kellogg is the most appropriate school for my purposes. It offers an outstanding department in my specialization—marketing—and a broad-based, flexible program to allow me to investigate other business disciplines. I have always excelled in group efforts, and Kellogg features teamwork in many of its classes. I recently spent a day at the Kellogg campus, attended a marketing class and met some students. I was very impressed by the friendly atmosphere in which bright, direct men and women were working together to meet their goals. It is an environment in which I will actively participate and thrive.

■ Analysis

Let's compare these two essays by looking closely at the stylistic and content characteristics of both. Perhaps the first thing that comes to mind in comparing these two essays is the differences in style. Essay #1 takes a very literary approach and uses a more elegant style of writing. Essay #2 is short and to the point, without complexity. This is style in itself! Both are very well-written, and both communicate well-thought-out and fully developed ideas in a smooth and logical progression. Both essays have very strong introductions. Essay #1 begins with a quote from a noted novelist. This quote provides both an eye-catching beginning and an excellent thesis for the essay. The writer obviously took a great deal of time to find a quote that related directly to the importance of having a purpose in life and career. Essay #2 answers the question in a single sentence. The reader is given an instant framework within which the essay's ideas are developed. Both essays have strong bodies—the question is answered using specific experiences to justify any and all assertions. Both essays contain strong conclusions. Essay #1 reiterates the main theme and ends with an extremely positive note. Essay #2, as well, ends on an up beat, reinforcing in the reader's mind the obvious enthusiasm of the writer. It is quite interesting to note how two completely different styles of writing can communicate in an equally effective manner while providing the reader with an insight into the different personalities of the writers.

These two essays have much in common in the way of content. Each applicant has spent the time to think through his or her reasons for getting an MBA, and each is able then to easily convince the reader of these reasons. Both applicants support their reasons with specific experiences, relating these experiences to their desire to pursue an MBA. Both applicants seem to have reached a stopping point in their present positions, wishing to gain the skills necessary to handle new and more advanced projects and careers. While both writers successfully accomplish their goal of convincing the reader that each requires an MBA to further their careers, Essay Writer #1 goes a step further than Essay Writer #2 by inherently demonstrating why he or she might be *more* valuable with an MBA than *other applicants*. Notice how each essay is a persuasive and convincing argument. The reader gets a clear sense of each stage in the evolution of the writers' lives and their career and educational decisions; a well-formulated career plan is presented in each case. Notice how both essays meet all five success criteria discussed earlier in this chapter.

In conclusion, the "You, the MBA, and Your Career" genre of essay is one which you will be faced with writing no matter what school you're applying to. You should write this essay for each school first, as it is the most important. It should be the easiest to write, given that you've thoroughly thought through your own "blueprint for success"—all you have to do is put your thoughts down on paper clearly and convince the committee of your conviction. Remember to apply Criterion #1—Clarity of Purpose—and be able to answer all of the questions associated with it to your essay.

"Substantial Achievements or Accomplishments"

This category of essay requires you to relate to the committee from one to three situations or experiences which you view as personal or professional achievements or accomplishments. You can bank on getting this question, in one form or another, on virtually every application. Here are just a few examples:

> *Describe your three most substantial accomplishments and explain why you view them as such. (Harvard)*
>
> *Discuss the three experiences which have most significantly affected the development of your career goals. (Wharton)*
>
> *Tell us about those experiences that have significantly shaped who you are today. (Stanford)*
>
> *Describe your most valued accomplishment and why you view it as such. (Kellogg)*
>
> *Describe two achievements of which you are most proud and the reasons for your satisfaction with them. (NYU)*

The importance of this essay often is underestimated by prospective MBAs. The answers you give to this question type are very telling to an admissions officer, as they provide the committee with an excellent view of what "makes you tick," what gives you a sense of pride and achievement, and what motivates you to achieve success. You must carefully think through your answer to this essay.

The first step in answering this question must be deciding what to include as an accomplishment or achievement. Let's begin with a definition of "accomplishment" and "achievement"—the terms are synonymous for our purposes. A good definition for both terms is: "an event or situation in which you successfully exerted control, resulting in a sense of personal satisfaction, which in turn allowed you to learn something about yourself, and which contributed to your desire to get your MBA." So, there are four questions to ask yourself when picking an achievement:

Did you affect the turn of events in some situation?

Did this outcome give you a sense of personal pride, success, and satisfaction?

Did you make a self-discovery?

Did this self-discovery influence your decision to get an MBA?

As you can see, there are many unwritten and hidden aspects to this deceptive and rather multi-faceted question. Few applicants are aware of the requirements of this essay. Far too much effort is spent on the part of far too many applicants in trying incorrectly to impress the admissions committee. The goal here *is* to impress the committee, though not with the achievement itself, but rather with why you were proud of accomplishing what you did. The objective magnitude of your achievements is nowhere near as important as the self-awareness gained through the experience. Most applicants worry too much about impressing the committee with largely unbelievable and newsworthy accomplishments. Always remember two things: (1) the committee will not be rating or judging your stated accomplishments on an objective scale, nor will they objectively compare your achievements to those of other applicants; and (2) you're trying always to convince the committee that you *need* an MBA—if your achievements are too wonderful and earth-shattering, you will inadvertently be saying to the committee, "I'm already so great that I really don't need an MBA from your school." Again, your task here is to provide the committee with a close look at your growth and self-awareness gained through your achievements. The sense of *why* you consider a certain accomplishment to be substantial is all-important. There are no good or bad achievements, and no one's accomplishment is better than anyone else's. Refrain from asking yourself, "Is this achievement worthy enough for XYZ school?" Refrain from exaggeration—honesty is always most impressive—yet be justifiably proud of your achievements.

As a practical strategy, make sure to cover three distinct areas when discussing any achievement: (1) a straightforward and detailed description of the situation or event; (2) why you consider it a significant achievement, and why you derived a sense of pride and satisfaction from it; and (3) how this experience contributed to your desire and decision to pursue your MBA. The latter is not specifically asked, but a good essay will touch on it. Remember, an undercurrent of "Why the MBA?" must flow through each essay. Let's look at some sample responses:

■ Response #1

As it has been said, a war is not won with one battle and so neither is my potential for success indicated by one accomplishment. For many people, there is often one event that stands out as the beginning of a life pattern. For me it was the sounding of my alarm clock the morning after being elected president of my *college fraternity. It may seem slightly odd that after four years in the business world I choose this event instead of something within the context of my professional experience, but the way Pi Kappa Alpha operates is certainly unlike most fraternities. What I faced that first morning and each morning for the next year was 135 men, a $60,000 annual budget, two fraternity houses and an advisory board composed of the national fraternity president and the Vice Provost of the University. My role as president was to oversee the executive committee, conduct weekly fraternity meetings, represent the fraternity on the House Corporation (a committee established to oversee the two fraternity houses and investment of excess chapter monies and endowments), coordinate the 15 in-house committees and represent the fraternity at all University functions. During the ensuing 12 months the fraternity successfully negotiated the purchase of a second fraternity house for investment purposes, endowed two student scholarships, raised over $8,000 for the Muscular Dystrophy Association and was selected as one of the top eight chapters in the nation (out of 135).*

In January of 1988, after working for E.F. Hutton & Company for three years as an investment banking associate in Public Finance, I accepted a position with Ehrlich Bober & Company as assistant to the Managing Director of Investment Banking. Following a number of years of market expansion and growth, Ehrlich Bober was experiencing a slow-down in business, as was the entire tax-exempt market due to the Tax Reform Act of 1986. My responsibility was to oversee the coordination and development of new management information reports including trading profit and loss, investment banking revenue projections, cost analysis and new business studies.

During the ensuing seven months, I coordinated the first firmwide computerized revenue projections in the firm's 20-year history, completed three regional new business studies and reorganized the antiquated profit and loss reporting system. After only seven months, the goals established for my position were complete and I was asked to return to investment banking to work with the Managing Director in establishing new business.

Of all my experiences to date, the one which I feel most clearly reflects my potential for success involved a financing for the City of Bridgeport, Connecticut in January of this year. The financing alone is not significant because I have been involved in over two dozen such financings during the past four years. What is significant about this particular project was the complexity of the situation and my role in completing the project. After a number of years of mismanagement and overly aggressive tax collection policies, the city of Bridgeport was placed in a state of fiscal emergency by the State of Connecticut after it was discovered that the City had accumulated a general fund deficit of over $52 million. Ehrlich Bober's role in this situation was two-fold: to work with a financial advisor appointed by the State to develop a long-term financial plan and to successfully finance the City's accumulated deficit with tax-exempt debt. My role, as part of a two-man team assigned to the account, included drafting all presentation material for the State's Financial Review Board, acting as a technical resource in the negotiations between the State and City regarding the State's guarantee for a portion of the debt, coordinating the drafting of the Official Statement and assisting in divestiture studies of the city's capital assets.

Thankfully, the eventual outcome for Bridgeport has been positive. With our help the City has successfully financed its accumulated deficit with long-term debt, and we are proceeding with the sale of certain city assets that will provide additional long-term capital and free up a number of Bridgeport's overextended resources. I hold this success as a personal accomplishment as well as a professional one. I can reflect on the past three months and know that my expertise and diligence will have a positive effect on the residents of Bridgeport. In the final analysis, my potential for success can be measured by this example, as well as by the others described above. However, I do not intend to have my potential for success measured by one particular event but rather by a trail of successes. Bridgeport is certainly not the end of this trail, nor is business school. My challenges and successes will continue as I develop the abilities and credentials to face new situations. I am poised and ready.

■ Response #2

My most valued accomplishment is having established a formal marketing department at my present company, PHH Neville Lewis.

Before I arrived, this office interior design firm had grown and prospered under the leadership of its founder, Neville Lewis. When the firm was sold to PHH Corporation in 1987, Mr. Lewis' role in the office diminished. We needed a marketing structure to replace his personality as the basis for generating new revenues. Furthermore, the interiors industry was becoming increasingly competitive and specialized. Our future depended on our ability to systematically identify and attract new clients.

As marketing coordinator, I was responsible for setting up this organized marketing program. I outlined an internal action plan based on immediate and long-term needs and then executed it. Within six months I had accomplished (1) compiling a comprehensive archive of the firm's 200 projects, descriptive and quantitative in nature; (2) updating and computerizing the company's qualifications—its services, staff and experience—into easily accessed records; (3) creating new marketing and sales tools—letters, mailers, mailing lists, newsletters, portfolios, slide presentations; (4) devising a data base lead-tracking system; (5) undertaking market research and competitor analysis; and (6) preparing a budget and cost analysis of marketing and sales activities. Due to my efforts, we immediately increased the volume of new business proposals from $1 million to $8 million and contract wins from 15% to 35%.

While implementing these new functions, I maintained other demanding responsibilities such as business proposals and public relations. I also contributed to the national marketing department of our new company. They specifically commended my work and sought my input on national marketing systems, communications and strategy.

This achievement is important to me because it has allowed me to improve my managerial skills. I trained and supervised a staff of diligent and motivated people. I have worked with the sales department and a wide variety of design professionals and senior management throughout the firm. I have learned more about the design industry and how good design can improve a company's efficiency and profitability. Thus I *can better identify and address our clients' specific needs. On my own initiative and with little formal training, I have successfully participated in a marketing venture. The experience reinforced my love of marketing as well.*

At the same time, this experience has shaped my desire to pursue graduate management education specializing in marketing. In that I was able to realize my own shortcomings in formal marketing knowledge.

With solid background in marketing theory, I know that I will be able to achieve even greater marketing accomplishments and successes in a services industry.

■ Analysis

Response #2 is a much more successful essay from the standpoint of addressing the three relevant issues alluded to earlier. Notice how Writer #2 is able to effectively and efficiently reveal more personality than Writer #1 by specifically discussing why the selected achievement was important to him or her, and how it influenced the MBA decision. Writer #1 takes a much more implicit approach, and the reader must "read between the lines" and use the mentioned accomplishments themselves to extract the writer's personality. While this may be viewed as merely a stylistic difference, it tends to put the burden of discovery on the reader—exactly where it shouldn't be placed.

What both writers have in common is an understandable and justifiable pride in their accomplishments, allowing the actual achievements to fade from importance in the essay.

Finally, keep in mind that the achievements you choose to discuss should reveal your uniqueness and individuality. Try to steer clear of achievements that are universally common among prospective MBAs, as this will detract from your individuality. For example, since every applicant is a college graduate, it does nothing whatsoever for your case to list among your achievements your graduation from undergraduate school, no matter how prestigious or demanding the program. The desire to do so is understandable enough, since each person is proud to have successfully completed an undergraduate education, and each applicant feels that his or her particular undergraduate experience was unique, but admissions officers tire of hearing about this achievement. The truth is, there just isn't that much difference between undergraduate programs. Furthermore, you'll be repeating information contained elsewhere on the application. Use a bit of common sense, and you'll be glad you opted not to be one of thousands claiming college degree completion as an achievement. Be a standout! Tell them something they don't *know about you.*

"*Leadership and Responsibility*"

Describe a situation or job in which you felt you had some responsibility and tell us what you learned from that experience. (Harvard)

Outside my job, I have demonstrated leadership by . . . (Wharton)

Discuss two or three situations in the past three years where you have taken a leadership role. How do these events demonstrate your managerial potential? (UCLA)

Describe a recent experience in which you exercised responsibility and judgment. What impact has it had on the development of your leadership skills? (Tuck)

This type of essay is included so that the committee can gauge your leadership and managerial potential. It is a close kin to the accomplishment/achievement essay, and in fact many applicants are unable to distinguish between the two. There is a big difference, though, between an accomplishment and a leadership role. Leadership, for purposes of your business school application, means *leading, managing and being responsible for people.* Examples might include offices held, positions in the community, projects involving delegation of authority and responsibility, and group leadership in the workplace. Recall that we defined an accomplishment as a *personal* achievement—some challenge you met which resulted in personal success, but not necessarily entailing leading a group of people. Think of it this way: All successful leadership positions are accomplishments, but not all accomplishments are leadership roles. Realizing the distinction between a personal achievement and a leadership and responsibility role will enable you to accurately and correctly answer the question. This distinction is especially important on those applications which require both an accomplishment/achievement essay and a leadership/responsibility essay. You should never use the same experience(s) to answer completely different questions.

Given that the major criterion defining and characterizing leadership and responsibility is managing people, your biggest task is to identify such a position from your experiences. Obviously, not everyone has assumed a position of leadership, office, or responsibility. If you don't have this type of experience in your background, you have two options: (1) apply to schools that don't specifically ask you this type of question (most selective schools, however, will want evidence of your leadership potential—you'll need to address the topic even if not specifically asked); or (2) put off applying until you have gained the necessary leadership experience. Top-level schools, remember, wish to train future business leaders, responsible people with great potential for success. If you have no related experience in your background, it will be very difficult to convince the committees of top schools of your potential, because you'll have no evidence to support your assertions of future management capabilities.

Like the accomplishment/achievement essay, three areas must be covered in the course of writing this essay: (1) a description of the leadership role or situation, (2) an explanation of what you learned or affirmed about yourself and your management potential through assuming this responsibility, and (3) the relationship between this self-discovery or reaffirmation and your desire to get your MBA. Again, as in the accomplishment essay and all essays, the latter area is usually the unstated question within the question. Let's look at a sample response to the Harvard leadership/responsibility essay.

■ **Response**

My most challenging work-related problem was assuming a leadership role in a complex public relations campaign I executed at AC&R Public Relations.

I was the youngest account executive when I joined the agency in late 1984. My first assignment was to create, present, budget and implement a four-month nationwide promotional *tour for Britannia children's clothing company, a new division of Health-tex, Inc. The campaign was challenging for several reasons. With its $400,000 cost, it was Britannia's entire 1985 promotion budget. It had to achieve many client objectives, including (1) introducing Britannia to the children's market, (2) positioning the clothes as fun, upbeat and spirited, (3) promoting the line to their own sales force, and (4) convincing stores to stock, re-order and promote the clothes. As a major new business segment, Britannia represented a sizeable investment for Health-tex. I was under great pressure to make the launch a success and keep safe a long-term AC&R account.*

The campaign itself was logistically intricate. A team of "freestylers"—trick bicyclists—were to perform in 30 shopping malls in 22 cities in 14 weeks. The multi-pronged p.r. and promotion program would include for each of these cities:

Media Publicity: *newspapers, consumer and trade magazines, TV, and radio publicity. I would write all press kit materials, produce a Britannia freestyle video for prospective press, compile media lists and secure coverage.*

Radio Promotion: *tie-ins and contest giveaways to be secured and administered.*

Community Relations: *children's modeling contests and bicycle safety lectures to be scheduled and coordinated, local youth organizations to be notified.*

Collateral Materials: *Britannia tour t-shirts, caps, balloons, booklets, posters—I would supervise design, production, and distribution.*

Mall Promotions: *Shipping display items and Britannia clothes, arranging bicycle raffles.*

Once I sold the campaign to the client, I undertook the mammoth task of implementing it in the only logical way—systematically. First, I established a schedule based on the client's priorities and a realistic itinerary for the team (kicking off in California and ending up in New York on Labor Day). I then contracted a mall consultant to negotiate with the malls. This difficult phase of the project took over a month. Simultaneously, I developed a budget listing costs by category, city and quantity. Only then could I start designing the media kits and collateral items. To help manage the vast detail and follow-up work, I assembled a project team to whom I assigned specific tasks. We met regularly to review progress, identify potential problems and resolve emergencies. I established distinct project procedures with the client, reporting weekly on the schedule and budget. I also sent weekly memos, meeting minutes, and wrap-up reports to the client, the appropriate regional Britannia rep, the mall and department store staff, and my account supervisors at AC&R.

Because of my careful planning and project management, the Britannia tour was an overwhelming success. We reached all our initial goals—extensive media coverage, healthy attendance levels, strong clothing sales and increased awareness of the Britannia name. The client was satisfied and elected to renew our contract.

The campaign was a personal triumph as well. I learned important management tasks—how to organize a difficult project into workable components, delegate responsibilities and monitor a complex schedule and budget. My communications skills improved vastly. I not only deftly pitched the event to major news and entertainment editors throughout the country, I *also negotiated with harried department store personnel and skeptical community representatives. This was the most expensive and important project of my public relations career, and it prepared me for even more significant responsibilities in the future. At the same time, however, I realized in dealing with my project team that I lacked some important people management skills. Although my team worked together in a successful fashion, I now know that I must learn more about management technique and leadership skills. I look forward to even greater success upon gaining the formal knowledge of management, planning and organization at Harvard Business School.*

■ Analysis

The writer of this essay has successfully written an excellent and winning leadership essay. He or she has taken the time to analyze the question and provide a thorough answer. The essay works on all levels, and the reader walks away with a true indication of the writer's present management capacity and future leadership potential.

Furthermore, no questions (for example, "What did this person learn from the experience?" "How did this experience impact upon the person's MBA decision?") are left unanswered in the mind of the reader. Remember, your ultimate goal in each essay, no matter the topic, is to thoroughly persuade your readers to admit you to their school; if questions linger on their minds, you've failed to completely convince them. Remember to cover the three relevant parts to this type of question, and your essay will be successful.

"Self-Analysis"

Many, but not all, applications ask you to describe those traits you consider to be personal strengths and those that you'd most like to change or improve upon (weaknesses—but the word "weakness" is seldom used). Admissions committees are once again trying to get a sense of you as a person. Here are some examples of essays in this category:

> *Which of your character traits do you consider your strengths? Which would you most like to change or improve? (Harvard)*
>
> *The area in which I have most tried to improve myself is... (Wharton)*
>
> *People describe me as... (Wharton)*
>
> *Please give a brief, candid evaluation of yourself. Include some discussion of the abilities and other attributes you believe are your strengths and some discussion of areas that you would like to develop more fully. How do others perceive you? What do you consider most unique or distinctive about yourself?* or *If a hypothetical business school admissions committee were to select its applicants without regard to an applicant's academic record or GMAT score, what would be the most compelling reasons to admit you? Be specific. (UCLA)*

It is best to be brief, honest, and pragmatic in your approach to this essay. Long-winded descriptions of numerous strengths and weaknesses are boring. Pick two or, at most, three of what you consider to be your outstanding personal strengths, along with a weakness or two (it's best to have more strengths than weaknesses), and concentrate on these.

Careful thought will allow you to narrow your undoubtedly numerous strengths to a few significant ones. The problem for most applicants is in deciding what to include as a weakness or trait they'd like to improve upon. The real trick here, and what will make your essay a success, is to relate your weaknesses to your desire to get an MBA. In other words, doesn't it make perfect sense to list weaknesses that can be overcome in the course of gaining your MBA at the particular school to which you're applying? Not only is this an honest and pragmatic solution, but it reinforces the answer to the unwritten question running through all essays of, "Why the MBA?" Isn't it true that you lack some sort of educational, theoretical, and/or analytical skill or ability? Isn't that part of your reason(s) to get an MBA? So, take this opportunity to elaborate on this aspect of your need to obtain your MBA. You'll simultaneously accomplish the goals of answering the question honestly and insightfully while advancing your argument for admission. It is the rare applicant who (until now, of course) is able to identify the key to this essay without some assistance.

Far too many prospective MBAs try the age-old tactic of couching actual strengths as weakness; this usually results in eye-rolling on the part of most experienced admissions officers who are easily able to read through such assertions.

Weakness such as "I'm much too thorough, too much of a perfectionist," "I have little patience for those less intelligent than I," "I work too hard," and "I'm an overachiever" usually get put into the "Give me a break!" file by the committees. Steer clear of this flawed and commonly used strategy, or you will probably only damage an otherwise excellent application.

Common sense dictates that you not list serious character flaws as weaknesses. You probably wouldn't want to describe your kleptomania, violent temper, or chronic lying to the admissions committee. Let's look at sample responses to the two Wharton essays.

■ **Response #1 (weakness)**
In the simplest terms, the area in which I have most tried to improve myself is in my variety of experience. In addition to my two summer internships, my first two years of relevant work experience was as an associate in municipal investment banking. Because I worked in the firm's New York office and because of the incredible volume of municipal business during this period, I gained a tremendous amount of experience within a short period of time. But regardless of how valuable I felt the depth of my experience was, nothing could prepare me for the turmoil that occurred in the markets nationwide during the fall and winter of 1987. As I quickly learned, it did not matter how extensive the skills and experience I had obtained were, my primary shortcoming was the lack of diversity in my work experience. I have attempted, within the last year, to correct that deficiency by accepting a position as the assistant to the head of investment banking at a municipal banking boutique. While this new challenge has provided me with a great deal of insight into the various aspects of managing a firm, it has provided only a limited amount of true diversification. I have therefore concluded that, at this point in my career, the only way to comprehensively provide myself with a broad base of business knowledge that can be used in both private industry and public policy management is to earn a graduate degree in

business. I have decided that governmental management is where my interests lie, but the dilemma I face is how to most effectively transfer my experience to that arena without becoming embroiled in the political structure. By being exposed to the many varied disciplines of a graduate degree, I am certain I can effectively make the transition to the public sector.

■ Analysis

This essay meets all of the criteria for a successful answer. The writer has picked a single weakness, one which enables advancement of his or her case and reinforces the need for an MBA. This writer is effectively clear in purpose and expression, uses specifics to back up the claim, and is brief in the description. Good answer, good answer!

■ Response #2 (strength)

I think most people make a determination about others based upon two very separate concepts: what they accomplish and how they accomplish it. Although very similar on the surface, these two criteria often provide a very different viewpoint of the same individual.

What a person accomplishes is a very objective, measurable concept. Whether I complete a project on time and successfully or whether the firm wins an account is an absolute result. Either I accomplished it or I did not. In my case I think that my accomplishments are without question. I have always been described as an achiever: voted "Most Likely to Succeed" and "Outstanding Greek" in college, promoted to the senior associate at my firm. People see me as someone who meets the challenges presented to him and accomplished his goals.

The second part of the equation, however, is a little more difficult to quantify: how have I accomplished my goals? This determination, in my opinion, is the most important. Throughout my adult life, the closest friendships I have and those I value most are those which started through a work experience or club activity. People view me as someone who can work both as a manager or "elbow to elbow" in the thick of things and yet still come away from the experience without alienating people or bruising feelings or egos. Regardless of the task before me, people see me maintaining both my integrity and my sense of humor. When all is said and done, this is the determination I value most.

■ Analysis

The writer has wisely chosen two outstanding and characteristic strengths to discuss, and she or he is able to convince the reader that if they were to meet face-to-face, the reader would walk away not only wanting to work with the writer on a professional basis, but would have an overwhelming sense of confidence in the writer's ability to get the job done. Thus, the writer's goal of conveying personal strength, in the context of career and future, has been accomplished in an effective and efficient manner.

Finally, this essay is yet another opportunity for you to distinguish yourself from the pack. Be sure to discuss the strengths and weaknesses you feel will make you a standout. Each person has unique strengths and weaknesses, yet not everyone is clever enough to discuss those very qualities. Take this chance to make your reader react with, "Hmmm... that's different," rather than, "Oh, no! Not another...." Be sure to end on a positive note; discuss a strength last if you're writing a single essay covering both strengths and weaknesses, or discuss how enthusiastically you look forward to improving yourself at the reader's school.

"Ethical Dilemmas"

In an age where unethical business behavior is prevalent, the top business schools are beginning to undertake to improve the situation by attempting to gauge the moral and ethical makeup of prospective MBAs. Two applications presently include this type of question—Harvard's and Stanford's. The questions differ, and are as follows:

Describe an ethical dilemma you have experienced. Discuss how you managed the situation. (Harvard)

Describe an ethical dilemma that you have personally encountered. What alternative actions did you consider and why? Do NOT tell us what you decided to do. (For purposes of this question, ethical is defined as "in accordance with accepted principles of conduct.") (Stanford)

Note that Harvard is interested in how you handled the dilemma, Stanford is not. Stanford's approach seems to be much more fair; be that as it may, the difficulties and intricacies inherent to both must be discussed.

Before you can begin to relate an ethical dilemma you've faced, you must be clear as to what is meant by "ethical" and what the committees are seeking to measure by the answers they receive. Stanford offers a definition of "ethical," but the definition really doesn't help the applicant in any practical way. The biggest mistake made in answering these questions is to confuse the terms "legal" and "ethical." For our purposes, a legal issue is not an ethical issue, and vice versa. What the committee seeks to determine is this: In a situation where it is unclear what is right or wrong—an unlegislated area where no official lines of conduct have been drawn—how far would you go? Where would *you* draw the line? They seek to measure your ethical judgment of what is right and wrong for you in a business or professional environment. Insider trading is not an ethical issue, it's a legal one. Failing to comply with the terms of a contract is not an ethical issue, it's a legal one. The issue of whether or not to embezzle funds is not an ethical issue, it's a legal one. If you are faced with these actions, you're facing legal issues—if you've committed any of these acts, you've broken the law. Yet, 90 percent of all applicants answer the essay dealing with a legal issue. Steer clear of situations that have clearly marked boundaries of behavior.

Let's look at an example of a response to the Harvard essay.

■ Response

I own and manage a shoe shine company which places attendants throughout New York and New Jersey. Recently we were scheduled to begin service at a very large suburban corporate center one hour from New York City, and difficult to access.

To fill the position, I hired a very nice man from Ghana who was willing to relocate to a town close to the center. In order to prepare him for the job, I had him work as an apprentice at one of our Manhattan locations (the Marriott Marquis) for a period of two weeks. He proved to be a model employee—he learned fast, and was both punctual and courteous at all times.

On the day he was sent to his new location, the building manager refused to accept him to fill the position. Our man had not even been given the chance to prove himself on the job. When I called the building manager, he claimed that he could not understand our employee, that our employee did not speak English, and that he (the manager) wished we had sent him someone who looked a little more "American."

Thus, I found myself faced with a tough ethical dilemma, which was whether to go ahead and comply with my client's demands and keep the account, or to forfeit the account in favor of my own personal feelings of right and wrong. I certainly felt that the client was wrong and acting in a discriminatory way. I realize that in a service industry, the customer is always right, but there are times one needs to stop and ask how far will he or she go to make a sale. Although this was an important account, I decided to cancel it. Our man from Ghana is now working at the CBS studios in Manhattan, where he shines Ed Bradley's and Dan Rather's shoes every day. Strangely enough, neither have any problem understanding him!

I must say that I surprised myself with my decision. Our company is young and growing, and only recently "in the black." Realizing that the bottom line is not everything to me, I feel confident that my ethical judgment will carry me far in the business world. I realize also that many more difficult dilemmas exist in the realm of big business and commerce, and I will need to learn more about business ethics and good judgment. I welcome the opportunity to participate in HBS's required "Managerial Decision Making and Ethical Values" course.

■ Analysis

It is evident that the writer was faced with a decision in which personal and ethical judgment were the only dictates of behavior. There were no rules or laws to guide the actions, only the writer's own sense of what was right and wrong. The decision was essentially between "the bottom line" and loyalty to the writer's employees and conscience. Not only is this dilemma classically perfect—the human factor versus the profit factor—but the ultimate decision effectively conveys the writer's personal sense of business ethics and judgment. Additionally, the reader gets a sense of the writer's self-discovery through the experience. The writer then relates the experience to the reader's school, always a wise move.

Ethical Dilemma questions pose problems for most people for a variety of reasons. The biggest problem most applicants face is the very existence of, and exposure to, an ethical dilemma. The admissions committees of both Stanford and Harvard incorrectly and unfairly assume that everyone has had to face an ethical dilemma at some point in his or her life. Perhaps their aim is to admit only those who have been working long enough to gain this type of experience; this is understandable, as these types of experiences certainly mature a person. What if you've been fortunate enough to have avoided ethical dilemmas up to this point in your professional life? Your next best choice, then, should be to examine your personal life. You may find that you're bombarded with ethical dilemmas every day! Have you padded your expense account at lunch? Should you inform your boss as to another employee's misdeeds? One applicant recently wrote an innovative essay on the unethicalness involved in personal relationships.

Another wrote of the ethical dilemma posed by job interviewing—for example, should one indulge in being wined and dined by a company when another job offer has been accepted? At some point in your personal or professional life, there is sure to be an instance or situation where you've found yourself wondering, "What's the right thing to do?" It's a safe bet that with any decision in which you've felt a twinge of discomfort or guilt, you've been faced with an ethical dilemma. Instincts are everything! Use these!

If you're absolutely at a loss for an ethical dilemma, and you're dead set on Harvard or Stanford, your approach may have to be one of, "I have been fortunate enough to have avoided ethical dilemmas; however, I can envision the potential for such a dilemma in the following situation . . . ," and go on to explain what you mean, and how you would approach the situation. Try to pick a hypothetical situation that is close to your present or past experience. With a little bit of memory searching and imagination, though, you should be able to come up with at least one event or situation that presented you with an ethical problem.

Be sure to note the differences between the requirements of the Harvard essay as opposed to those of the Stanford essay. In writing the Harvard essay, a three-pronged approach is best, as shown by the sample response: Describe the situation, discuss how you dealt with the problem, and tell the committee briefly what you gained from the experience. As with all essays, being honest is always the best policy; however, in answering the Harvard ethical essay, be sure to discuss a dilemma in which your course of action ultimately shows good instincts and judgment. Although the reader may not be judging you as a good or bad person, distinctly unethical behavior may leave inquiring minds wondering.

Since Stanford wishes not to hear of your dilemma resolution, you needn't worry or concern yourself with revealing your ultimate decision to the committee. In writing the Stanford essay, simply describe the dilemma, give the committee a detailed look at your thought process in evaluating the situation—citing specific alternative courses of action and why you might consider each one—and relate anything you may have learned about yourself or business management in analyzing your ethical dilemma.

Finally, you may want to consider saving this essay until last. Ethical dilemmas are touchy subjects, and certainly quite difficult to write about. Finish the more mainstream essays first, saving time to ponder your eventual approach to the ethical dilemma essays.

"For Fun"

While every school includes space for listing hobbies and extracurricular activities, only the more selective schools will ask you to discuss these activities in an essay. Many applicants wonder why an academic admissions committee is even interested in what you do for kicks. Be assured that this is indeed a very important essay and one not to be neglected or taken lightly. How you spend your time away from the office is one of the best ways for the committee to learn about you as a person. Explaining to the committee why certain activities are important or appeal to you allows them to get to know you in a more familiar way and enables them to see what makes you tick. Further, it allows them to get a feel for how well you'll fit in with other students and how you'll contribute to the social life of the school. The two years you spend at business school will be a very social existence, and student-student interaction is quite important. There are very definite strategies for answering this type of question. Examples of essays in this category are:

Describe your avocations and hobbies. (Harvard)

For fun I . . . (Wharton)

What leisure and/or community activities do you particularly enjoy? Please discuss their importance in your life. (UCLA)

What do you do for fun? (Chicago)

What are your special interests and how have these interests contributed to your development? What interest(s) would you pursue if financial support or time considerations were not a factor? (Duke)

What are your principal interests outside of your job or school? How do they appeal to you?(Tuck)

Imagine that you have just been transferred to a remote city that has very little to offer in the way of cultural activities or entertainment and you will have to fill your non-working hours with activities of your own creation. What would you choose to take, and what would you do to occupy your leisure time? (You may not choose to work extra hours.)(NYU)

The immediate reaction of most applicants is to want to list every activity known to man: "I love to bike, swim, run, ski, golf, play tennis, play racquetball, hike, go to the theater, attend concerts, collect stamps, all watersports, etc., etc., etc...." This "shotgun" approach misses the point of the essay completely! You won't get points for having the most extracurricular activities; it's not a contest. What you must realize is that this type of essay provides you with the ultimate opportunity to present yourself as a unique individual. Capitalize on it! Here's your strategy: First, pick one or two activities to talk about. Think of an empty, lazy Sunday. You've nothing but time on your hands. What would you most like to do with that time? That's the activity you'll discuss, because that's the one thing you love to do most, and your discussion will be focused, enthusiastic, and enlightening without much effort. By discussing your *favorite* extracurricular activity, you'll automatically be setting yourself apart from other applicants, because most won't share your love of that very activity, and if they do, their reasons for enjoying it will be different than yours. Second, go into detail about your activity. Talk about the feeling you get when you participate, and why you like that particular activity. Tell the committee why this activity is important to you—give them a very personal view of you on your "down time," with your shirtsleeves rolled up, in your jeans and t-shirt. Of course, it doesn't hurt to have that rare activity that sets you apart automatically (one young woman recently related her love of hunting with a bow and arrow); however, don't fictionalize a favorite activity, because your delivery won't be sincere enough. Again, be honest! The activity itself takes second place to your detailed personal feelings about it. For example, another young woman (28 years old) related how she loved to go to baseball games with her father. Ever since she was a little girl, she would go to games with her dad, wearing her baseball cap and taking her glove. The reader got a wonderful sense of the importance of this activity to the writer.

As an aside, note that the NYU essay is very creative in form. Take advantage of this—be equally creative in your response. Two recent applicants took very different approaches for their essays. One wrote a letter to his best friend, informing him of being transferred, and relating how he planned to restore a 1965 Ford Mustang in his spare time. Each phase of the restoration was described, so that the reader got a good look at an activity that truly appealed to the writer. The other applicant wrote her essay in the form of a journal entry—writing to her diary about being transferred, and how this would give her the opportunity to do something she was unable to do in the city. She described how she would plant a garden, going into detail about different growing seasons and planting techniques. Both essays were quite successful.

Let's look at two examples of the "for fun" essay.

■ Response #1

For me, the one thing that brings the most enjoyment and the most fun is the pursuit of antiques. But antiques as a broad classification is not altogether accurate. I have never had the financial resources or desire to deal in rare and expensive pieces of furniture or art. The area which I find most fascinating is that which I call day-to-day trash and treasure. For as long as I can remember, the opportunity to comb through mounds of knick-knacks and other old junk has been a treat. My treasures are more of what were once a part of everyday life. I usually limit my hunts to objects from the period of time between the birth of my grandparents and my own birth. This as-

sures me a point of reference or at least someone to provide the final word for those unexplainable devices. One of my favorites is a cast iron object I found several years ago at a flea market. To me it looked more like a medieval torture device than a usable utensil. After some research at the library and discussions with older relatives, I discovered it to be a bread toaster once used on an open-hearth fireplace!

The value or the rarity of the objects that find their way into my collection has never been important to me. The real joy is in the process of discovery, both at the shop or market and of the object's original use. I think true fascination is the understanding of everyday life during the 75 years before my birth.

They say that one man's trash is another man's treasure, and I certainly provide the treasure part of the equation and just maybe a better understanding of everyday life during the late 19th and early 20th century.

■ Response #2

I have always felt that my special interests and activities outside of work were not a separate section of my life to be considered if time permits. My attitude lends itself more to the thought that what I do at work and the activities and interests that fill my time out of the office have an equal impact on who I am as a person, as well as upon each other. With regard to what I do outside of work, these activities and interests can be divided into two very separate groups: organized special interests and good old-fashioned fun.

For my entire adult life there have been several organizations which hold some special significance for me. I have a tendency to become involved in a few organizations and remain active for a number of years as opposed to finding new, trendy interests every few months. The organizations I am active in have, at some point in my life, contributed to the type of person I am and helped lead to my achievements. One such organization is the Boy Scouts of America. When I was eleven, several of my friends joined the Scouts and after some persuading, I joined as well. What began as mere peer pressure developed into a lifelong affiliation. After obtaining Eagle at 14, I became somewhat disinterested for several years only to find myself back involved as an adult leader in a local Troop during college. During that time, I feel I actively contributed to the development and maturation of several young men, but more importantly, I was able to reassess what the Boy Scouts had provided me as a teen: an understanding of responsibility, an appreciation for the outdoors, an opportunity to experience a number of new and varied interests, and a solid foundation on which to build. I have not forgotten those lessons learned as a Scout leader and have since remained involved through raising money and acting as a community advisor for a Troop in New York. If nothing else, my current role in the Scouts gives me an opportunity to put back into an organization a portion of the benefits it provided me when I was younger. That satisfaction encourages me to continue to contribute to the development of my community.

My life has always been filled with plans, organizations and a generally structured lifestyle. However, this certainly is not a conscious intention, it is merely the way I am with most things. I guess that is why the free time I reserve for myself (Structure — here we go again!) is filled with spontaneous activities. Of all the things I do, both inside and outside of work, the time that brings the most enjoyment and relaxation is the time I spend with my wife. I have always made a conscious effort to do things that do not require committee approval or a written plan when I'm with her. Spontaneity is our motto. The time spent with her provides me with tremendous pleasure, as well as a release from everyday tensions and concerns. It never seems to make much difference what we do.

As I mentioned earlier, the activities in which I am involved are important to me, and are an integral part of my personality and my hopes for the future. With this in mind, if I had no time considerations or financial concerns, the organizations I am involved with and activities I pursue would not be any different. What would change, however, is the amount of time and effort I devote to these pursuits. In the case of the Boy Scouts, I would devote substantially more time to developing Scouting for inner-city boys and girls. As for those things which I do purely for myself—spending time with my wife and enjoying my hobbies—these could not be improved on by any amount of money or with any less time constraints. They just do not get any better.

■ **Analysis**

There's no mistaking the distinctly different and uniquely interesting personalities and personal lives of these two applicants. On the basis of this alone, the essays are successful. Note how each writer is unafraid to let the reader share in his or her enthusiasm for the chosen leisure and community activities. (Stylistic differences and length of response can be accounted for by noting that the first essay responds to the Wharton question, while the second responds to the Duke essay.) Note also that each writer is careful to be very detailed in describing not only the actual activity, but in relating to the reader his or her personal feelings about the activities.

As you think and begin to write about your leisure time, try to allow your reader to share in your interest, enthusiasm, and passions. Imagine you're talking to one of your close friends; trust your reader with your feelings and personality. If you approach this essay in this manner, you'll be sure to have an attentive and interested audience!

Other Essay Types

A. "Painful or Difficult Experiences"

A close kin to the ethical dilemma, this type of essay is a bit more lenient in that the definition of "painful" or "difficult" is entirely subjective. The admissions committees will be much more interested in what you learned from whatever experience you discuss, and how it relates to and impacts on your decision to go to business school, than in what the actual experience was. The essay is included in order to provide the committee with a look at another type of experience in your background. If this question wasn't asked, your application would probably be void of difficult experiences, unless of course you're asked to relate an ethical dilemma. At present, though, only Stanford and Kellogg ask this type of question. Once again, the three-pronged approach is the best strategy: describe the experience, discuss what you discovered about business management and/or yourself, and conclude with noting the relevance of this experience in your MBA decision. Kellogg's and Stanford's questions appear as follows:

Discuss (in 500 words or less) a difficult or painful experience from which you learned (what you consider to be) a valuable lesson. (Stanford)

Discuss a difficult professional experience from which you learned a valuable lesson. (Kellogg)

■ Response

The following case describes a mishandled corporate acquisition and the important management lesson I learned from it.

In April 1987 PHH Corporation (NYSE: PHH), a Fortune 100 services corporation, bought Neville Lewis Associates, an office interior design firm. PHH merged NLA with three other design groups to form the second largest organization in the country. They paid a high price for NLA which was operating at its all-time highest level of revenue and profit. Unfortunately, PHH Neville Lewis (as the firm was now called) experienced sudden and severe business reversals. The October 1987 stock market crash eliminated 75% of its client base—the financial services industry. At the same time, most of its projects were under construction and there was no backlog to replace them. The firm desperately needed new business, but its existing customers were financially strapped and prospective clients were wary of the new ownership.

PHH's solution did not alleviate the crisis. They immediately cut operating costs by firing nearly half of the staff and eliminating year-end bonuses (even though most of the year had been strong). Mr. Lewis, who as President had always pro-

vided leadership and stability, was assigned to a "shuttle diplomacy" role of supervising design in the New York, Washington, Philadelphia, and Dallas offices. Thus he could neither use his reputation to attract new business in New York nor by his presence improve office morale. In an act of desperation, PHH hired two salesmen with no contacts or expertise in the industry to make cold calls on sophisticated and demanding clients. The salesmen were well-intentioned but ineffective. As a result, the office lost top talent and potential clients, who spotted trouble. By February 1988, morale and workload were at an all-time low.

PHH had taken the wrong approach because it didn't understand the office design business. They didn't recognize that design is a people-intensive business. When you alienate and lose quality staff, you cannot easily replace them. Therefore, you lose your ability to deliver quality services. PHH also misunderstood the customers. When making a design decision, clients are committing millions of their companies' to a design firm. Thus a firm's reputation is critical to its success. When word of PHH Neville Lewis' internal disorder spread throughout the industry, potential clients were naturally reluctant to hire them. Additionally, PHH had never analyzed the historically cyclical nature of design. It is a business extremely sensitive to shifts in business and corporate favor. Thus, PHH Neville Lewis' 1987 income was not necessarily representative of its consistent earning power. By setting unrealistic targets based on atypical numbers, PHH placed additional pressure on the firm when it was unprepared to perform.

Lack of marketing expertise exacerbated the lack of new business. PHH neglected to structure an integrated marketing plan (based on knowledge of the industry) for attracting and retaining clients, improving service offerings and communicating with employees, clients and the public. My boss and I seized this opportunity to establish a new marketing program which I then implemented over the next six months. As a result, we strengthened our staff, regained credibility in the industry, and increased business opportunities.

This experience has shown me what is needed in a company to manage change and prosper over the long term. First, you must understand the nature of your business. What works for car leasing (PHH's core business) does not apply to selling design services. Managers must understand the product or service they are offering, then plan, budget and implement accordingly. Second, you must respect your employees. By underestimating the backbone of its new company, its human resources, PHH undermined its ability to produce. People need responsibility, opportunity and rewards to continue to grow and contribute to their organization. Third, you must provide leadership. Companies assume the character of their managers. When Neville Lewis ran his company, his strengths and values spread throughout the office. His love for design and respect for his staff inspired them to strive for excellence. By contrast, if the top person fails to articulate a corporate mission, a harmful void will ensue. Only when Mr. Lewis and the New York Managing Principal devised and expressed a new vision for PHH Neville Lewis' future did the company regain its former strength.

This experience proved to be a turning point in my career as well. I determined that I want to direct companies towards healthy futures, during stable or changing business circumstances. I enjoy the process of analyzing situations and devising creative solutions to problems through effective marketing and management.

B. "Creative Brainbenders"

Given your current employer and given the opportunity to effect one change, what would that be? How would you implement the change? (Harvard)

Discuss the vocations or professions, other than administration, which you may have seriously considered. (Harvard)

What roles do the ability to function in a team environment and strong interpersonal and communication skills play in providing leadership in the business community? (Chicago)

Alfred Whitehead once said, "Great men and women of business think greatly of their functions." In your view, what is this function? (Columbia)

Discuss your views regarding the management of technological change as a vital skill for future managers, what impact technological change has had on your chosen career field, and how study at MIT will prepare you to face these challenges. (Sloan)

Expert mastery of new technologies and knowledge of the rest of the world are clearly not the only keys to managerial success—managers must be able to persuade organizations that they must change to meet the challenges of the future. Describe a situation you encountered in your employment or educational experience that required organizational change. Tell how you would effect that change as the manager in charge and what skills you expect to learn at MIT to help you accomplish such change. (Sloan)

These questions are designed by admissions committees in an attempt to understand your perception of the world around you, how you think, and how you see yourself fitting into that world. What you have to say is important, but more important is *how* you say it. The committee wants to experience your brain at work—they want to see "how your wheels turn upstairs." Thus, your strategy is to present an honest and original, well-reasoned idea, and back that idea up with a sound logical argument, using specifics as evidence. Again, clarity of expression and purpose are very important. These essays provide yet another opportunity to express your individuality, as each applicant will say something different from the next. Attempt to provide the admissions committee with a fresh idea, and your essay will be mostly successful.

C. "Academics"

Harvard and some other schools (notably Columbia) ask, "What evidence can you present to demonstrate your capacity to perform well academically in the Harvard MBA program?" As a practical strategy in approaching this question, first take into consideration the academic environment of the school posing the question. For example, it would make most sense to target your Harvard essay towards the case method of study, since Harvard's teaching is entirely case method. Rather than generally pointing out how well you performed in college (a strategy most people employ), try instead discussing a specific course in which a bit of the Socratic method (learning through example and discussion) was used, and offer your performance and enjoyment of this particular class as evidence of your ability to handle Harvard academics. Keeping in mind two of the mandatory essay techniques of being specific and relating all experiences to your desire to get an MBA, this approach makes sense.

D. The "Optional" Essay

Almost every application will give the applicant the "option" to add something further to the application. NYU puts it this way:

> *Please provide any additional information, which the application has not given you the opportunity to include, that you feel is appropriate and relevant. Topics may include comments about previous academic efforts, any special interests or other accomplishments you would like to bring to the Admissions Committee's attention, or comments on any physical, emotional, or family difficulties that you have encountered that should be known to ensure a fair evaluation of you. If you are unable to submit an evaluation from a current employer, please give your reason here."*

If there's one thing that the "optional" essay is *not*, it's optional! No single application (with the possible exception of Harvard's, and they don't offer an optional essay) at present provides the applicant the chance to cover all the aspects of his or her life. *Never omit the optional essay!* Take the opportunity to reinforce and advance your persuasive argument for being admitted to that school. The NYU optional essay contains many good ideas for topics. You may wish to borrow an essay from another application if you feel it's an important aspect of your background to bring up. If there's any relevant aspect not covered in a particular application, use this time to cover it.

Most applicants, it must be revealed, discuss deficient grades and/or GMAT scores in this space. Not only is this monotonous for the committee, but it calls attention to the weak points of your application. Opinions vary on this subject, however, and you must make an individual determination on whether to discuss poor grades or low scores. On the one hand, an applicant with excellent work experience, great essays, sterling recommendations, superior GMAT scores, but inferior grades may wish to explain this inconsistency, feeling that this will leave no questions in the mind of the committee. On the other hand, why direct attention to the weak link, especially when grades are only one factor in the application? If you do feel compelled to use the optional essay to discuss grades and GMAT scores, take a positive, persuasive, and offensive approach to the essay, rather than making defensive excuses. In other words, rather than offer up reasons for low grades and scores, convince the committee that the other aspects of your application should weigh more heavily in the admissions decision. A defensive stance does nothing for your case. Finally, be sure never to repeat information contained in other parts of the application, and always end on a positive note. Here is an example of an excellent "optional" essay:

■ **Response**

Within this envelope is the most comprehensive package of information ever assembled about me. I have never had the opportunity nor the reason to put together such a package, and in reflecting on the "experience," I come away with a certain amount of satisfaction. I have learned a great deal about my-

self, both by looking back at my accomplishments and academic records and by looking forward at my hopes, dreams, and aspirations.

After putting a great deal of thought into this application the one thing that has become self-evident is that no one part of this package adequately describes who I am and what I wish for the future. To look at my recommendations or work experience or academic record or extracurricular activities singularly does not describe my potential in the business world or why I should be admitted to Wharton. However, the thing that each of these individual pieces tells when taken together is that I have a history of success at each phase of my life. There is no doubt in my mind that this point in my life is not the end of that potential. The question for me now is "can I succeed and reach my aspirations without a graduate degree?" My answer to that thought is an emphatic "NO!" As my work experience and activities indicate, I have never wished to merely participate. With this in mind, my next step is to earn the credentials, analytical skills, broaden horizons and general maturation that comes with an MBA.

For me, that "step" is achieved at Wharton. After spending a few days visiting classes, talking to professors and students and spending a great deal of time studying what other programs have to offer, I have come to realize that Wharton has the most to offer me in preparing for the future. It is with these thoughts in mind that I offer to you my application for admission and an individual ready to assume the rigors and challenges of Wharton.

Conclusion

The success of a journey is measured not only by the number of miles crossed, but by the new perspectives gained along the way. If you keep this thought in mind when answering the many essay questions that will face you, you will have the proper frame of mind. Writing essays to business school applications is an intensely introspective and exhausting experience. The rewards, however, are tremendous.

To conclude this most important chapter, keep the following hints in mind:
- Take your time, and take the essays seriously.
- Be honest in your approach.
- Market yourself as a valuable addition to the school.
- Be aggressive in content and style (persuade them that they *need* you).
- Make yourself stand out. Toot your horn (be proud of who you are and what you've achieved).
- Keep essays on point and interesting.
- Make your applications look professional—use a computer word processing package.

8

Letters of Reference

In this chapter, we'll be covering three questions: whom should you ask to write a recommendation, what should a good reference letter say, and how should you go about asking for one. Keep in mind three letters—easy ones—A, B, C. They stand for the three qualities your recommendations should address: Academic ability, Business know-how, and Character.

It is not expected that each recommender will be able to attest to all factors. Ideally, one should be able to examine your intellectual performance, and another should be able to analyze your ability to interact in a business situation. If a third reference letter is requested, you might consider someone who could address your personality and character (including such traits as creativity, loyalty, determination, imagination, and sense of humor).

Whom Should You Ask to Recommend You?

Someone who knows you *very well!* Someone who will write a *good* letter for you! A good letter is one which *positively and specifically* reinforces what you've said about yourself in your essays. Many applicants have a tendency to think that a letter from a prominent or influential person would be the best type of recommendation. In reality, this generally isn't true. This type of recommendation often results in a generic, "he's a credit to his community" letter that provides no information about *you*. Further, it does nothing to advance your case with the committee; remember, the components to your application must be designed to persuade the committee to accept you. When the committee receives what appears to be an orchestrated barrage of such letters for one candidate, the overall effect can be modestly negative. If a number of similar letters from alumni, prominent people, and various unconnected personages appear in a folder, committee members feel as if they are being manipulated, and they have to fight a little harder to remain objective.

The ideal person to attest to your academic or intellectual ability is a former professor (or current one if you are still taking courses). Your choice should be someone with whom you had extensive contact and for whom you did outstanding work. The professor should be able to deal with questions concerning the breadth of your academic interests, your research methods, your analytical ability, and your written and oral communications skills. This person should also be able to compare your academic ability and performance with those of other students the professor has taught. Thesis advisors, major subject professors, and independent study or research advisors are good examples of whom you should approach for academic references.

Many applicants prefer to use undergraduate activity advisors (coaches or counselors, for example) as their recommenders because they've developed a much closer relationship with these advisors than with any of their professors. Be careful! Remember, you want someone to attest to your analytical and intellectual ability. An advisor for a sport or the student government might not have had that type of relationship with you. Reference letters are quite specific—the questions asked are specific, and recommenders are always asked about the nature of their relationship with you. If you want the admissions committee to weigh the recommendation seriously, you must make sure that the people you've chosen have extensive information about you in the capacity for which they are writing the letter of reference.

For applicants who have been out of college for some time, or who never developed a close relationship with a professor, finding an academic reference will be difficult (but not impossible). Many applicants have been out of school for quite some time and have not been in contact with their college professors for years. It is likely that your professors may not remember you. Further, even if they do remember you, your current abilities may be very different from your college abilities.

Other sources of academic reference letters include professors or instructors of postundergraduate classes (such as graduate courses or extension courses) and training seminar leaders. Many people take graduate courses in nondegree programs or general studies courses. If you've taken such a class, you may be able to find a professor or instructor who could write the recommendation. Many companies provide on-site training courses and send employees to seminars at universities and conference centers. If you've attended a training seminar and had the opportunity to develop a relationship with one of the teachers, then that teacher or seminar leader might be an excellent source for an intellectual reference.

If you have had no formal academic work since college, the best approach is to select a colleague who has had the opportunity to observe your analytical and intellectual abilities. Ask the person to concentrate on those aspects of your character.

An admissions committee needs to have some idea of your capacity to do rigorous intellectual work. But proof of that ability need not come from your undergraduate college. In fact, as was discussed in Chapter 6, the longer you've been out of school, the less important your college work becomes, and the more important your business experience becomes.

Your second letter of reference should be from a professional business colleague, preferably your current supervisor. Your professional or business recommender should be able to deal with issues such as your ability to analyze a problem and find a viable solution, your maturity, your self-confidence in business dealings, your creativity, and your management potential. (The last is a vague term; however, a person who is a success in business knows the characteristics that make for success and should be able to recognize them in others.) Some schools even inquire as to the applicant's sense of humor, an invaluable asset in making it through the rigorous demands of an MBA program.

It is, at times, inconvenient to ask your present supervisor or employer for a letter of recommendation. This is especially true in situations where you don't wish to have your employer know of your plans to leave the company for a full-time MBA program. For many, this presents an ethical dilemma, especially in the case of the prospective MBA who has made a commitment to the firm. Admissions committees are quite aware of this difficulty. If you absolutely cannot get a recommendation from your current employer, your strategy then is two-pronged: first, ask a former employer to write your professional recommendation; second, inform the admissions committee of your inability to secure a letter of reference from your present employer in the optional essay (as discussed in Chapter 7).

If you are unable to secure any business recommendations because your experience is limited, don't apply at this time. While it is necessary to establish your academic credentials, your ability to function in a complex business situation is much more important to most MBA admissions committees.

One final word on the topic of whom to ask: while the essential idea is that the recommender should know you very well, a prominent person *who knows you very well* is even better. Again, the letter must not be a generic endorsement. A well-written and specific letter from an assistant professor is much better than a general note from the Secretary of Education in Washington, D.C. However, if the Secretary of Education writes a very specific letter about how you prepared for him the most comprehensive research report he's ever read, and goes on to cite examples of the quality of the report, you'll have secured the ideal letter of reference.

What Should a Good Reference Letter Say?

Above all, a letter of reference must paint a realistic picture of you and highlight the reasons why you are an excellent candidate for an MBA. Recommenders should try to relate your abilities to the study of business administration and the skills needed by business leaders. A good recommendation discusses your "unique" qualities—those qualities that separate you from all the other applicants who have similar credentials. Each point should be backed up with specific references to things you have accomplished. It is not particularly helpful to say only that a candidate was an outstanding student.

Your recommendation must address the needs of the particular school as well. Thus, the recommender must know the school's teaching emphasis and mission statement. If it is a theoretical school, the letter might address your quantitative abilities. If it is a case method school, the letter might address your broad conceptual skills. It would be a complete disaster if the letter for Harvard addressed your quantitative skills while the letter for Chicago or MIT addressed your general management skills.

Admissions committees appreciate candor, and no letter should attempt to portray an idealized picture of you. On the other hand, letters which contain negative comments or portray you in a substantially different way than you've described yourself in your essays may be damaging, even if they are honest. Since you have complete control over whom you ask to write your letters, it shows lack of business judgment if you select someone who does not hold you in the highest esteem.

As a purely practical strategy, a separate letter on the recommender's letterhead should be attached to the recommendation form. Each school includes in the application package its own recommendation form with specific rating grids and questions to be answered. It shows a real concern and interest on the part of the recommender if a separately written letter is attached to the form; this will then reflect very favorably on you. The attached letter should not reiterate, but rather embellish upon the qualities you possess that were not addressed in the form letter.

The admissions committee will use the information provided to make judgments about you; it is also possible that they will use the letters to draw inferences about you. The caliber of the recommender, the amount of time and thought that has gone into the recommendations—these are all reflective of you. Make sure they reflect well.

How to Make a Recommendation Request

The approach taken in asking someone to write a letter of reference for you is an important consideration, yet one which is mostly overlooked by most applicants. How a recommender is asked may directly influence the outcome of the letter.

Ideally, a request should be made in person. Remember that you are asking someone to put in a great deal of effort on your behalf. Make it as easy as possible for that person. This also means that you do as much of the work as possible: *you* supply the stamped, addressed envelopes, *you* fill out the objective data on the recommendation forms, *you* supply résumés and samples of your work, *you* supply background information about the specific interests of each school that you are applying to, and you do so *in person*, if at all possible. The worst way to make the request is by simply calling the person on the telephone.

If the person lives a great distance from you, then send a letter and include a photograph to make sure that there is no confusion about who you are. It is also a good idea to (as alluded to above) include a copy of your résumé or copies of work done under the supervision of the recommender. This is especially relevant if you have had no contact with the person for some time. No matter how outstanding your work was, things fade from the memory with time. The more ammunition you provide to the recommender, the more likely it is that the recommendation will be specific and forceful.

Always clue your recommender in as to what should be included in the letter. Try to determine if that person will write a good letter for you and whether she or he is willing to write and attach a separate letter to the recommendation form. Many times, in the case of professional business recommendations, the target recommender simply doesn't have the time. If this is the case, seek another recommender. If, on the other hand, your recommender has no time, but asks you to draft the letter, then by all means do so! Keep in mind what makes a good letter—be positive, persuasive, and forceful. Include specific examples for every generalization you make. It is always possible for the recommender to tone down the letter, but it is unlikely that the recommender will be more positive than you are.

If your recommender shows the letter to you before it is sealed in the envelope, you may be faced with an ethical dilemma. According to the law, you have the right to inspect all of your academic records. Many graduate schools of business include on the recommendation forms they use a space advising you of this right and asking you if you wish to waive this right so that the recommendation can be considered confidential. This is a tricky issue. You do not want something negative in your file, yet both recommenders and admissions committees seem to be more comfortable knowing that you did not read the letter of reference. Of course, some schools do not make confidentiality an issue. If so, then by all means take a look at what the recommender has said.

A week before the recommendations are due, call the people who are writing them and make sure that they are aware of the deadline and are still willing to write the recommendation for you. It's too late once the deadline is passed to find out that illness or pressing business obligations precluded writing the letter. Better safe than sorry.

As a courtesy to your recommenders, write them a thank-you note. This, unfortunately, is a lost art, but one which is greatly appreciated. Much time and effort has been spent on you, and your recommenders deserve your thanks. If a note is beyond you, use the phone, but do say thanks. Once you make your final decision about where to attend business school, it would be nice to inform all your recommenders of the final result of their efforts. This holds true even if you are not accepted to the school(s) of your choice. If the MBA is right for you, you may be reapplying and will continue to need their support. Anyone who has played a few innings of the game is entitled to know the final score.

Conclusion

On a more practical note, you will want to organize the process of securing letters of reference. In Appendix B you will find a reprint of a Letters of Recommendation Organizer. Fill out one of these for each of the schools to which you are applying. Make sure that you note the purpose of each recommendation: Is this person attesting to your academic ability, your business skill, your character, or your self-discipline? This way you can be sure that every aspect of your candidacy is covered for every school.

There should be a Letters of Recommendation Organizer for each school to which you apply, so duplicate as many of them as you need. In some cases, the names will be the same for all the schools. In any case, fill out one for each school, and be specific about its purpose. If you are careful with files, the application process will be greatly facilitated. When all the pertinent papers for a specific application are in one place, the chances of forgetting something important diminish.

9

Acing the GMAT

Hundreds of GMAT test preparatory books line the reference shelves of bookstores, while dozens of test preparation centers advertise daily in newspapers all over the country. No question, the GMAT is big business, and the question of how best to prepare for the GMAT is a difficult one. In this chapter, this and other questions will be discussed and answered. Topics such as test preparation methods, standardized test-taking strategies, and maximizing your GMAT scores will be covered. Keep in mind, however, that this discussion is by no means meant to compete with or replace any preparatory method or material, nor is it meant to be a comprehensive and definitive treatise on taking the exam.

What Is the GMAT?

The GMAT (Graduate Management Admissions Test) is one of several standardized entrance examinations written and published by Educational Testing Service (ETS). The test is administered four times each year by the Graduate Management Admissions Council (GMAC)—in January, March, June, and October. The testing schedule follows a standard academic year calendar, meaning that the first test of the year is in October. You should be aware that most of the top business schools prefer you take either the October or January exam. This is basically because of the lengthy score reporting period, approximately six weeks. Most application deadlines occur in March or April, and a March test score will not reach the admissions committee until May. Plan on taking either the October or January exam. To register for the GMAT, you must get a copy of *The GMAT Bulletin of Information* from ETS; you can do so by calling them directly at (609)771-7590, or by picking up a copy at any nearby college or university career office.

The GMAT is a standardized, 3½-hour, 7-section, 135-question, multiple-choice test. Each of the seven sections is 30 minutes in length; the number of questions varies from section to section. Each question offers five choices from which you must pick the best possible answer. Of the seven sections, only six are scored; one test section is experimental and does not figure into your score. It is included in order to pretest questions that will someday be scored. Unfortunately, this section cannot be distinguished from the others, so each section must be taken as if it were a scored section.

Of the six scored sections, three are mathematical and three are qualitative, or "verbal," in nature. Math sections test your ability to reason and solve quantitative problems. Verbal sections test your ability to understand and evaluate reading material and to recognize basic elements of English.

Verbal Skills

The three sections testing verbal skills break down into Reading Comprehension, Critical Reasoning, and Sentence Correction, accounting for 70 questions. Let's take a brief look at each section, starting with Reading Comprehension.

Reading Comprehension

If you've ever taken a standardized entrance exam before (such as the SAT), you've had to struggle through a reading comprehension section. GMAT Reading Comprehension is like reading comprehension on any other standardized test you've taken. It is the bane of nearly everyone's testing existence. You'll be faced with 25 questions in this section, distributed among three 500-word (approximately) reading passages. You'll see one passage from the natural sciences, one from the social sciences, and one from the humanities. The only element they have in common is that they are all dry, dense, boring, and not the kind of thing you'd read if given your choice. You must work quickly and accurately to score well on this section. The questions basically measure your ability to understand, analyze, and apply information and concepts contained in the passages. All of the questions are to be answered on the basis of the passage, so you need no previous or specific knowledge of the material. There are six basic question types in Reading Comprehension.

The first and perhaps easiest type of question tests your ability to grasp the "big picture," or main thesis, of the passage. A second question type asks you to draw an inference from facts and implications made in the passage—"reading between the lines," if you will. Yet a third type of question tests your ability to understand the logical relationships between the important points and ideas in the reading passage; for example, you'll be asked to determine the strong and/or weak points of the author's presentation. A fourth type of question requires you to locate and interpret details, facts, and statements made in the passage. A fifth type of question will test your ability to apply the main idea of the passage to another situation—to extrapolate. Finally, you will be asked to characterize the author's writing style and tone.

Critical Reasoning

Close on the heels of Reading Comprehension in similarity is Critical Reasoning, a relatively new addition to the GMAT. It entails using many of the same skills used in Reading Comprehension, but concentrates more on reasoning skills and the logical structure of a short argument (in Reading Comprehension, you are given much longer "arguments" and asked a wider variety of questions). The 20 questions in this section test your ability to critically read, make, and evaluate arguments. Most of the questions are based on a separate argument, debate, short reading passage, or set of logical statements. Most of the material is drawn from the realm of business in an attempt to gauge your facility with material similar in nature to what you'll be faced with in business school. From this standpoint alone, most test takers find this section easier to handle and somewhat enjoyable, compared to Reading Comprehension.

Two basic types of questions exist in the Critical Reasoning section. The first consists of questions regarding logical argument construction. You'll be asked to recognize and identify the basic structure of an argument, properly drawn conclusions, underlying assumptions, and parallels in reasoning. The second type of question will test your ability to evaluate the logic of a particular argument or piece of reasoning and to recognize factors that would strengthen or weaken the argument (in much the same way as was mentioned in the discussion of Reading Comprehension question types), reasoning errors made in constructing an argument, and aspects of the argumentative methodology.

Sentence Correction

Sentence Correction may be viewed simply as a 25-question quiz on standard written English and is basically an editing exercise. The questions require you to be familiar with stylistic conventions and grammatical rules and to demonstrate your ability to improve ineffective or incorrect written expressions. The goal of the test evaluator here is to gauge your writing ability.

In each question, you get a sentence, part or all of which is underlined. If an error in grammar or style exists, it will occur in the underlined portion of the sentence. Five different versions of the underlined portion of the sentence are offered as answer choices, and your task is to pick the choice that does the very best job of expressing the intended meaning of the original sentence.

Once you learn what ETS considers a good sentence, you've got this section beat. A good sentence, in the eyes of ETS, has two broad characteristics: correct expression and effective expression. A *correct* expression is grammatically and structurally sound. It conforms to all the rules of standard written English, like subject-verb agreement, noun-pronoun agreement, verb tense, pronoun case, and consistency. An *effective* sentence expresses an idea or relationship clearly and concisely, as well as grammatically. This means that there are no superfluous words or needlessly complicated constructions in the best choice. (This does not mean, however, that the choice with the fewest or simplest words is necessarily the best choice.) Also, effective expressions use proper diction—you must be able to recognize whether the words are well chosen, accurate, and suitable for the context of the sentence.

Math Skills

The math half of the test consists of two sections of Problem Solving and one of Data Sufficiency, accounting for a total of 65 math questions.

Problem Solving

The two 20-question Problem Solving sections are perhaps the most straightforward part of the GMAT: you're given a math problem and asked to solve it. About half of the questions are in a straight mathematical setting, and the rest are verbal "real world" word problems. GMAT math covers arithmetic, elementary algebra, and geometry—nothing beyond ninth-grade math. This is good news and bad news for most people. On the one hand, it is comforting to know that the concepts tested are very basic; on the other hand, trying to recall and refresh one's junior high school math memory can be a battle in itself.

Data Sufficiency

The third math section is called Data Sufficiency, and the name says it all. The 25 questions in this section test your ability to analyze a quantitative problem and to determine when enough relevant information exists to solve that problem. It's a bit of "fun with numbers"—logic and math at the same time. Math is the concept, logic is the format. This section is much different from all other sections in design. Your task is not to answer the actual question asked, but to classify the questions according to predefined classification categories. In this section, the "answers" are all predefined; that is, answer choice (A) always has the same predefined meaning, (B) always has the same predefined meaning, and so on. In Data Sufficiency, answers (A) through (E) predefine varying degrees of sufficiency classifications. The section is what ETS terms a "fixed format." Again, instead of answering the actual question posed, as in all other sections of the test, you must classify the additional, supporting information given as being (A), (B), (C), (D), or (E), according to the predefined classifications.

That concludes the structural overview of the GMAT.

How Is the GMAT Scored?

The overall GMAT score is on a scale of 200 to 800, with 800 being the highest. Few people score over 700 or below 350. In addition to the overall scaled score, you'll receive two scaled scores for Math and Verbal, each on a scale of about 1 to 60. Scoring the GMAT is a three-step process. First, a raw score is computed. Very simply, you are given one point for every correct answer. Each question is worth the same amount. A quarter point is deducted for wrong answers, and nothing is deducted for omitted answers. This quarter-point deduction is a random guessing penalty. For example, if you were to randomly guess at answers, over the course of thousands of questions you should get one out of every five correct, since there are five answer choices in each question. That means your raw score would be zero—one point for the correct answer, minus one-fourth of four (incorrect answers), or one, totalling zero. So, any advantage gained by random guessing is eliminated by instituting this guessing penalty. More on the issue of guessing will follow in the strategy section of this chapter.

The next step is to calculate an adjusted raw score. Once your raw score has been calculated, ETS statistically adjusts and equates your test to an objective equation, thereby eliminating any advantage or disadvantage gained by taking one version of the test over another. In other words, if ETS determines that the January test was objectively more difficult than the October test (based on answer statistics and distribution), the January test taker needs a lower adjusted raw score to attain the equivalent scaled score than does the October test taker. Therefore, it matters not that difficulty varies from test to test.

Finally, ETS sets your adjusted raw score to its 200 to 800 scale, and your Math and Verbal adjusted raw scores to their respective scales. If you've taken the GMAT before, your previous scores will also be reported, and an average given. Some schools will look at this average, some will look at the most recent score, and some will look at the highest score reported, thereby giving you the benefit of the doubt. Most top schools follow this prescription; some, however, have built-in adjustments for second-time GMAT testers. For instance, in order for Stanford to take your highest score into consideration, you must have increased your previous score by 40 points; otherwise, it is likely that the average will be used in the admissions process. This makes sense, because 40 points on the GMAT scale does not represent a large difference in actual percentage of correct answers obtained.

If you want confirmation on what a particular school does with your GMAT score, call the Office of Admissions at that school—they will usually give you a straightforward answer.

Preparation, Strategy, and Commonly Asked Questions

Must I prepare?
Yes, yes, yes, a thousand times yes! Even if you are extremely good at taking standardized tests, you must take the time to familiarize yourself with the idiosyncrasies of the GMAT. For most people, a preparation period of six to eight weeks is optimal, assuming at least two hours are spent each day preparing for the exam. One thing is certain: you will perform much better on the GMAT if you are at ease with the structure and nature of the test than if you risk taking it "cold."

What is the best way to prepare? Must I take an expensive preparation course?
There are two basic ways to prepare for the GMAT: on your own or by taking a preparation course. It is *not* necessary to spend hundreds of dollars on a preparation course! Prep

centers do one thing well, and that's play on the insecurities of prospective test takers. It is quite important for you to realize that test prep centers do not use actual GMAT material. They can't! GMAT tests are not disclosed, and they are copyrighted to prevent anyone from using them to profit by them. The material used at test prep centers is not written by professional test writers, but mostly by recent college math and English majors. The material only approximates the questions on the actual GMAT and is frequently inaccurate and outdated. All test prep centers do is to give you a bit of structure to your study and preparation. They are no substitute for hard work. Furthermore, many of the teachers at these centers have never taken a real GMAT, only the material written by the center. *It is not the same*! Test prep centers target students who feel they would be lost if they didn't have someone spoonfeeding them on how to take the test. If you feel you fall into this classification, you should seriously reconsider your goal of admission to a top MBA program. A student who is motivated enough and confident enough to feel she or he can handle the curriculum at a top school certainly doesn't need a commercial test prep course in order to ace the GMAT. At a going rate of over $600, the payoff is not worth it.

How then should you prepare? Your first step is to buy *The Official Guide to GMAT Review*. It is published each year by ETS—the people who write the GMAT—and is the *only* source of actual GMAT material. If you can, secure older editions as well. If you have friends who have taken the GMAT within the past three months, have them order a copy of their exam for you. This will give you the most recent GMAT to study with, and it is perfectly acceptable. In addition, purchase some of the commercial prep guides found in bookstores. You'll learn the same material (which is often better written than the unpublished material found in test prep centers) and save a great deal of money. You can supplement your study materials with commercial math and grammar reviews. This will round out your preparatory material. You are now ready to begin your preparation.

Before you get started, you must understand a few things about standardized test taking and preparation. Further, you must set specific goals based on these principles.

The first and most important thing to remember about studying to take a standardized test is, *"The test maker is always right!"* The sooner you realize this, the sooner you will be on your way to becoming a worthy test taker. Remember, your sole goal on the exam is to get a point out of each question. Realizing that the test maker is always right will enable you to adopt the proper frame of mind. Your goal is not to point out why you think your answer is better than the credited one, but to figure out why the test maker gave a point for the credited answer. You will be effectively turning the tables on the test maker! Think about it for a minute—the test maker has given you the credited answer, all you have to do is find it among the four decoys. This attitude requires a bit of intellectual humility and ego sublimation on your part, but it will allow you to perform well on the GMAT.

The second principle you must be aware of is that, although each question is worth the same amount (one point), they are not of equal difficulty. Those who score the highest on the GMAT realize this quickly and capitalize on it. You must be able to work through a given section of the test in such a fashion that allows you to gain the maximum score; this is done by answering the easy questions first, those of medium difficulty next, and so on. While there are some questions that are objectively easy (anyone can do them), it is far more likely that the terms "easy" and "difficult" will be subjective—what's easy for you may be difficult for someone else. The point is that you must, throughout the course of your preparation, constantly keep track of your individual strengths and weaknesses. Only by this qualitative approach will you truly become a wise test taker. It is not important what your score is on a practice section of some book, because no one cares. Not a business school in the world will ask you how you did in your GMAT preparation. The only score that counts is the one you get back from ETS, so steer clear of simply gauging your performance by bottom line scores. Keep noting the kinds of things you consistently get correct, the kinds of questions you struggle with, and the kinds of questions you cannot handle at all. In this way, when it comes time to take the test, you can work through a section answering questions that you're a pro at first, thereby ensuring a top score. It would be a disaster to simply answer the questions in the order presented, only to waste time and discover that you didn't get to the last 10 questions that were right up your alley. Good test takers never take the questions in the order presented, because it's never an advantage to do so. Again, learn your strengths and weaknesses so that you can avoid wasting time and can attain the maximum score you're capable of.

Closely related to this principle is the third: "*The GMAT rewards the mover, not the plodder.*" The point to be made here is that timing is important. You must make the effort in your study to move through the questions in a systematic fashion (as we just discussed) as quickly as you can. Make sure you divide your time wisely on a section, and stick to a schedule. Far too many test takers ignore timing. You must realize that *anyone* can do well on the test, given enough time! Knowing your strengths and weaknesses will be a great aid to you in shaving off precious seconds of time as you prepare. By test day, you should be able to glance at a question and know instantly whether or not to attempt it. You never want to find yourself 90 seconds into a math question (all that's allotted!) and discover that you can't do the problem! Once again, keep honing your timing, and make the attempt to look at every question in a section. How else will you know if you can do it or not?

The last GMAT principle to think about as you begin your study concerns guessing. Recall that a random guessing penalty exists. Never guess *randomly!* However, if you can eliminate some of the wrong answer choices, or even only one, the odds are in your favor. As you go through your practice, try to determine how good an educated guesser you are. Try to track your success and failure rate by the number of possible answer choices remaining. In other words, what percentage of the questions do you get right when you guess at one of two remaining possible answer choices?

This concludes our discussion of some of the things to keep in mind as you begin your GMAT preparation. If you keep these principles in mind, your assault on the GMAT should be a very effective one. As a structural suggestion, consider working on one section at a time, spending more time on those sections that give you the most trouble. In other words, don't practice taking full-length GMAT exams at first. Work on Reading Comprehension one day, Problem Solving the next, and so on. As you begin to understand where your inherent abilities lie, you can restructure your preparation so that more emphasis is placed on the weaker areas while the stronger areas are kept honed. Let's now examine some specific, section-by-section strategies.

What should my strategy be in Reading Comprehension?

The key strategy in Reading Comprehension lies in the ability to recognize and extract important and necessary information in an efficient and effective manner. As a starting point, consider why you normally read. Usually, it's either to learn something or for pleasure. Neither of these apply to GMAT Reading Comprehension. You have only one purpose to consider in this type of reading: getting a point for each question. Therefore, your reading must be adapted to the design of the section. The very worst thing one can do is simply read a passage in normal everyday fashion and then attempt to answer the questions. Consider the following points, and the rationale behind them:

1. Don't necessarily start with Passage #1.
You'll perform much better on passages with which you have some association, and the first passage may not be your best subject. For example, Passage #1 may be the humanities text. But if you were a science major in college, you may have a greater facility with the science passage. The material will be more familiar to you and your comprehension greater. Therefore, take a few seconds to glance at each passage before you actually begin your work, and plan an order of attack based on your own background.

2. Look at the questions accompanying the passage first.
Remember, your goal is to extract information that the

test maker thinks is important. Only the information required by the questions is of concern to you. What better way to structure your reading strategy than to have some idea of what you'll be asked? Spend about 15 seconds skimming the questions before actually starting to read the passage.

3. Read carefully until you locate the author's main point.

It almost always occurs in the first quarter of the passage. The main idea is the key that unlocks the passage. If you can't find it, you can't complete Reading Comprehension. Not only do a large percentage of questions directly and indirectly deal with the main idea, but correct answers to other questions will encompass and relate to the main idea. The main idea is the "big picture," so to speak—the point of which the person writing the passage wants to convince you. It will sum up the evidence and facts presented. Each passage has a main idea, either explicitly stated and implied. Whichever the case may be, find that idea or thesis as quickly as possible!

4. Don't read every word.

Once you find the main idea, the remainder of your reading should be a cursory mapping out of the structure of the passage. Try simply to get a general "feel" for the layout and development of the passage on a paragraph-by-paragraph basis. That way, you can refer back to the necessary paragraph and examine it in detail when working on a particular question. Far too many people waste time reading the passage carefully the first time through, underlining and taking notes as they go. Remember, you're *not* trying to learn anything! Simply noting the topic of each paragraph is far more beneficial, because it allows you to quickly locate reading material when and if you're required to do so by one of the questions. Don't memorize details—note their location and move on.

5. Don't waste time.
Underlining and note-taking wastes time. It gives you the illusion of getting something done. Mental paraphrasing is a much more effective strategy.

6. Don't spend more than 10 minutes on any passage.
Each passage has some easy questions attached to it, and you'll miss out on these easy points if you stubbornly waste time trying to answer more difficult questions.

What should my strategy be in Sentence Correction?

This section is very straightforward, so use this straightforward, five-step strategy based on the design of the section:

Step 1
Read the original sentence, identifying any flaws in grammar or style in the underlined portion. (Don't be predisposed to finding an error; about 20 percent of the questions have no errors.)

Step 2
Before looking at the answer choices, correct the errors as *you* would edit them.

Step 3
Look at all of the choices except (A)—it is a repeat of the original underlined portion, and to read it would be a waste of precious time.

Step 4
Pick the answer choice that represents the clearest, most concise, and most grammatically and stylistically correct expression of the original idea.

Step 5
Read the answer back into the original sentence. Don't neglect this step! Many times an answer choice may sound "correct" on its own, but when combined with the rest of the sentence becomes incorrect.

What should my strategy be in Critical Reasoning?
The strategies involved in this section are similar to those associated with Reading Comprehension. In this section, however, the emphasis is on logical argumentation. Therefore, your strategy must be to identify the logical structure underlying each argument. There are three components to a Critical Reasoning argument: evidence or supporting facts, a conclusion or main idea, and an underlying assumption that ties the supporting facts to the conclusion. This is no different from the structure of Reading Comprehension passages; it's simply easier to analyze with a shorter argument. All the questions will address one of these components, and with not much practice you'll become quite adept at identifying these components.

What should my strategy be in Problem Solving?

It is important for you to realize that GMAT math is much different than high school math. The GMAT math sections do not test knowledge of concepts as much as they test one's cleverness with a few basic concepts. The intuitive test taker will do much better than the number-cruncher. This means looking for the shortest, quickest route to the answer. Often, a quick glance at the answer choices before you begin blindly writing equations will provide you with all the insight you need. It is equally important for you to be aware of the various difficulty levels of math questions. Some are so easy that virtually anyone with a high school math background could answer them; some are very difficult. It is in the Problem Solving sections that your knowledge of your own strengths and weaknesses will really pay off. Remember to skip around within the section! Further, take no more than $1 1/2$ minutes on each question. This makes sense, as there are 20 questions given in 30 minutes.

What should my strategy be in Data Sufficiency?

The key strategy to be used in this section centers on method. A methodical approach will parallel the structured design of the section while minimizing the chance of error. The following straightforward method is quite effective:

Step 1

Determine what is being asked. Two types of questions exist in this section: a "yes or no" question, and a "calculation" question (for example, "Is Bob taller than Sue?" and "How tall is Bob?") An actual answer to the "yes or no" question will be yes or no. Calculation questions will have a number for an actual

answer. (Keep in mind that you are not really
concerned with actual answers—this step simply
provides a good starting point.)

Step 2
Spend a few seconds thinking about what kind of
information you need to answer the question. This will
aid you when you actually begin analyzing the
supplied information.

Step 3
Now you must analyze the two separate data
statements to decide whether or not they are sufficient
enough to yield one and only one answer to the
question. (This is the definition of "sufficient."
Information is insufficient if more than one answer to
the question is possible.) *Take the two given data
statements separately.* This is a key strategy, and one
ignored by most GMAT test takers. First, keeping data
statement #2 covered with your finger or pencil,
analyze data statement #1. Place a small "i" (for
insufficient) or "s" (for sufficient) immediately after
the data statement. Do the same with data statement
#2, keeping #1 covered. You must completely erase
data statement #1 from your mind when working with
#2! In most cases, you will have automatically
rendered the correct answer by this point.

Step 4
If you discover that you have two insufficient pieces of
data, you must now combine them to see if together
they provide an answer to the question.

There are three major errors made by test takers in this section:

1. *Being predisposed to finding an answer of "yes" to a "yes or no" question.* Many people confuse "sufficiency" with an actual answer of "yes." The two are not synonymous! Similarly, an answer of "no" does not mean "insufficient." "No" is a perfectly acceptable and sufficient answer to a "yes or no" question!
2. *Doing too much work.* Do only as much calculation and analysis as are needed to see that a single answer can or cannot be obtained. Remember, you are simply trying to classify the sufficiency of the supplied data statements; you are not trying to answer the question posed!
3. *Not following this common-sense method!* For example, many test takers will mistakenly keep data statement #1 in mind when analyzing data statement #2. This directly opposes the prescribed method and will most certainly lead to error.

Remember that you will be attempting to answer 25 questions in 30 minutes; therefore, you must work a bit more quickly in Data Sufficiency than in Problem Solving.

How should my final week of preparation be structured?

You've worked hard for over a month. You've got a good feel for the GMAT. You know the directions by heart. You know basically where your strengths and weaknesses lie, and your timing is good. It's a week before the GMAT—what else can you do? Plenty! Let's break down the last week into several segments: Sunday through Thursday night, Friday and "GMAT Eve," and Test Day (Saturday).

From Sunday through Thursday evening, your sole goal is to take "dry runs" at the exam, hone your timing, and set your mind to doing well. A good way to do this is to save four full-length sample GMATs from the books you bought for these four days. That way, you can take a full-length exam on each of the four weekdays, Monday through Thursday. Remember, up to this point, you've hopefully been working on the test on a section-by-section basis. This should be your first real attempt at full-length exams.

Before taking your first practice GMAT on Monday, reinforce in your own mind exactly where you stand with the test sections. A great way to do this is to set aside an hour or so on Sunday evening, grab a few sheets of paper, and do a little self-analysis in the following manner: At the top of each sheet of paper, make three columns—"Excellent," "Fair," and "Poor," or "Know it Cold," "Shaky," and "Alien." Do this for each section of the test. Down along the left hand side of the page, list the various concepts tested in that section. For example, for Reading Comprehension, you may want to list the six types of questions—main idea, facts, inference, logic, extrapolation, and tone. You might also list the three areas from which passages are drawn. Then, objectively as you can, rate yourself according to the top columns. The first column is reserved for the types of things you always get right; the second column is reserved for the types of questions that you can handle, but aren't your forte; the last column is reserved for the types of questions that always throw you. By doing this for each section (it's especially important for the math section to list all the various concepts tested), you can reinforce in your mind what you know and what you don't know. It's as important to know your weaknesses as it is to know your strengths, perhaps even more so. You must be able to glance at a question and immediately know whether or not to attempt it. You're now ready to take the four practice GMATs you've saved for the final week.

As you go through these tests, be very strict with your timing, and try to simulate "battle conditions"—go from section to section without stopping. Take a fifteen-minute break after the fourth section. If possible, take at least one practice test at nine in the morning. You'll be surprised at the difference time of day makes on your performance. If you're like most prospective MBAs, you'll have studied only at night. Your mind is much fresher in the morning, and you may be pleasantly surprised at your increased scoring performance. Remember, you're trying only to hone your test-taking style and to maximize your score. It's too late at this point to cram or study anything new. By now, you realize that the GMAT is an analytical test, not a test of recall and knowledge; therefore, you can't "cram" for the test even if you wanted to.

The last week before the test is also a period of decision making. Do you feel as ready as you'll ever be to take the GMAT? If the answer to this question is anything but an emphatic "yes," *don't take the test!* Well over half of your performance on this test will hinge on your confidence in your ability and your psychological preparedness. If you have doubts in your mind, you'll be constantly second-guessing yourself, which is disastrous on the GMAT. You must know what you know cold, and know what you don't know as well. It's more important to be psychologically and mentally ready to "ace the GMAT" than it is to be as physically prepared as you can be. That is, you can always have studied more. But, you must now believe that you'll never do better at another time. It's far better to take the GMAT once and do as well as you can do than it is to take the test once and perform only marginally and be forced to take the test again.

This week is also a time to get control of the test, not only from the aspect of actual test-taking practice, but also from an environmental aspect. In other words, take the time to visit your future test center to familiarize yourself with the space. You'll do better if you feel somewhat at ease with your testing environment. Find out where the bathrooms, vending machines, and phones are, what the seating arrangements are like, and how to get there. This sounds a bit silly, but it'll pay off. To relate a recent incident, a GMAT test taker did not take the time to locate the bathrooms before sitting down to take the test. At the break, she was forced to find it on her own. The bathroom was two floors up, requiring an elevator ride. By the time she found it and returned to the testing room, the proctor had started the second half of the test without her, and she lost valuable time.

Stop all of your GMAT work Thursday evening, in order to give your brain a good rest before the actual test. You will risk burnout unless you take this advice. Further, if you study on Friday, it's likely you'll find something that you've never seen before in your practice, and it will throw you psychologically. That will destroy your confidence. True, you run this same risk Monday through Thursday, but at least you'll have time to put it out of your mind by test day. Try to do as little as possible on Friday. If you can take the day off, do it—be as "brainless" and relaxed as you can be. On Friday evening before the test, get together everything you'll want to take with you: #2 pencils (take 10 sharpened ones), your GMAT ticket, at least one picture I.D., erasers (take a couple of differing hardness—you'll avoid tearing a hole in your answer sheet by doing this), a lunch (you can't rely on vending machines), change for the phone, several layers of clothing (you'll be taking the test in a public building or school on a Saturday morning—very rarely are the atmospheric conditions perfect; it's either too cold or too hot), a watch (don't take a beeper watch or a calculator watch—they're not allowed), earplugs (technically they're not allowed, but if you need quiet, the proctors almost always allow them), and something to read (to wake your mind up before the test, and for during the break—there is much "dead time" in the test, so try to keep the brain waves from fading!). Put all of this somewhere that you can pick it up quickly and easily on Saturday morning. Don't stay out late on Friday evening. Go to sleep early and set your alarm(s) to allow a leisurely morning.

On Test Day, have a good breakfast to provide energy for the rather exhausting morning, and get to the testing center at 8:00 a.m. This will allow enough time for you to "get there," that is, to feel at ease, relaxed, and ready for the test. If you didn't visit the center during the week, check the place out at this time. Follow the proctor's directions to the letter, and take the test just as you have been doing all along. You won't see anything new or different, and if you've prepared adequately, you'll do just fine. That's all there is to "acing the GMAT!"

Conclusion

If you think of this test as a matching of wits, a game with the test maker, the test and the mandatory preparation will be a fun process. If you think about it for a minute, that's all it really is! There's no one at ETS who's any smarter than you are, and all they've done is written some questions, supplied you with the answer, and tried to distract your attention away from the answer they want you to find. That's not too hard to do with a bit of practice. Have fun with the GMAT, and you'll do very well.

10

The Interview—A New Feature

Almost every business school states flatly that interviews are not part of the admissions process; however, a handful of schools now openly encourage interviews. Wharton, Kellogg, Cornell, and Tuck all now include an interview as part of the admissions process. You may also decide to seek an interview on your own even if it is not required. This chapter will prepare you for an interview by going over what you can realistically expect.

Should You Seek an Interview Even if It's Not Required?

People seek interviews for several reasons. Some feel that they interview well and that verbal communications skills are one of their strongest assets. If that's the case, an interview will probably strengthen their chances of admission. Another reason for an interview, and a much more pragmatic one, is to influence the admissions committee when they are put on the waiting list for admission. A final reason might be to seek information about the school—to find out firsthand if the school is right for them. If all you seek is information, then any representative of the school (usually a second-year student) will be able to provide that. But if your purpose is to advance the case for your admission, then you should attempt to speak with someone on the admissions committee. If you are traveling a long distance, it is especially important to make sure you will speak with a committee member. Some of the schools now requiring interviews use recent graduates or second-year students employed as graduate admissions assistant interviewers. Take the initiative and request to speak with a committee member.

What Types of Interviews Exist at Present?

There are two basic types of interviews: on-campus and off-campus interviews. With on-campus interviews, you're much more likely to be speaking with a member of the admissions staff. On-campus interviews should be your preference, if given the choice. The outcome of the interview is much more likely to advance your case.

Off-campus interviews are generally conducted by an alumnus of the school who lives and works in your area. The interview will be more relaxed (probably over lunch or dinner), and you'll find that you may have more in common with this type of interviewer. The only drawback is that this type of interview probably won't carry the same weight as an on-campus interview.

How Should You Prepare for the Interview?

Whichever type of interview you select, set up your own agenda. Remember that the interview should be used to introduce new material, not to rehash information already available on the application. You might take three sheets of paper and head them: "Major Theme," "New Evidence," and "General Impression." On the first sheet, state as succinctly as possible the one idea you wish to leave in the interviewer's mind after the session. On the second sheet, put down the new material that will support the theme and that you hope to work into the conversation. The general impression is harder to pinpoint. Ask yourself, at your best, how do people perceive you? Are you quiet and determined? Outgoing? A numbers person? People-oriented? Obviously your personality contains many of these disparate elements, but in a short interview you cannot convey every facet of your character. Select what you think are your best assets, and try to get those aspects of your nature across. The essential point is that you should work to control the interview, not let yourself be controlled by it.

Prepare yourself to meet many different types of interviewers. In general, you will meet well-trained, professional people, but occasionally you will find the interviewer using ploys that could create problems for you. One of these might be to use a series of rapid-fire questions, a tactic designed to put you off guard. Interviewers do this to see how you react under stressful conditions. The key to handling this type of situation is to try not to become rattled. If you have done your homework, you will know how to answer most of the questions thrown at you; if you don't know an answer, say so, and ask the interviewer to give you the answer. Ask a question of your own if you can. But never forget your basic theme. Try to work your theme and evidence into the conversation as much as possible. In this case, what you say is not as important as conveying the impression that you are able to stay cool under pressure, and to perform in an adequate, if not brilliant, fashion.

Another trick to prepare for is the use of chatty informality—interviewers who chat about the weather, sports, and anything seemingly aimless. What these interviewers seek to find out is if you can take control of a situation. Here again, your job is to get across the basic theme and evidence that you planned to present. You must bring the conversation back to your chances for admission and why you would make an ideal candidate. If you aren't prepared, you won't be able to take constructive control, and the interview will have been wasted and perhaps counterproductive. The interviewer may walk away with the idea that you do not have clearly defined objectives when you go into a meeting, and that you are not able to interact with others in order to achieve those objectives.

If you're really motivated, you can even rehearse a mock interview. Have a friend play the role of the interviewer, or rehearse in front of a mirror. Either way, you can see for yourself what impression you are making. The mirror is very effective for nonverbal behavior (you can examine posture, hands, eye contact), while the role-playing will give you the benefit of another person's reaction to your answers, behavior, and demeanor. You might want to try simply preparing some questions and answering them into a tape recorder. This is especially beneficial in judging your verbal presentation. Do you speak cogently on a given question or is your response a series of "umms"? Do you speak slowly and distinctly so that the interviewer can understand and appreciate what you are saying or are you talking at the speed of light in order to get through the question? Are you satisfied with your response?

Whatever you do, don't repeat yourself, and don't repeat the catalogue. The interviewer will most probably have read or been told the contents of your application and will expect that you have read the catalogue. If you ask questions that are already answered in the catalogue or volunteer information already covered in depth in your application, you may do more harm than good.

What Are Some Guidelines You Should Follow?

First, be conscious of how you look. Dress conservatively! Women should not take this opportunity to wear trendy clothing, and men should be well groomed. Your goal is to make an impression through your verbal interaction, not through your stylish dress. Treat the interview as a job interview.

Second, be aware of body language. Strive to maintain eye contact with your interviewer, as this exudes confidence and helps establish some rapport. It's a signal to your interviewer that you're a mature, well-adjusted person. Shake hands firmly with your interviewer, both upon greeting and upon parting ways, as this suggests self-confidence and an ability to handle social situations. Don't overdo it, though;

"meatgrinder" handshakes are not called for. Maintain good posture, and don't fidget, put your fingers in your mouth, play with your hair or nails, or constantly look at your watch. You don't want to come across as nervous or lacking in the social graces.

Third, strive to communicate positive personal characteristics. In other words, arrive slightly early, show respect and courtesy, exude energy and enthusiasm, end the interview on a positive note, and send a thank-you note. Sending a note shows good manners and thoughtfulness and leaves a positive impression on the interviewer. The note can be handwritten or typed—though handwritten is more socially correct and more personal—and can be very brief: "Dear XYZ; Thank you for your time last Friday afternoon, October 9. It was a pleasure to speak with you. I appreciate the information that you gave me about Harvard, and I look forward to hearing from the committee. Sincerely, Frank Lee Hopeful."

Keep the following rules in mind:

1. *Do not, under any circumstances:* smoke, tell jokes, respond in an arrogant manner, eat or drink in the interview, make patronizing or personal remarks about your interviewer, or argue with the interviewer. In other words, be on your best behavior.

2. *Even if the interviewer offers you a cup of coffee, refuse.* It's simply not appropriate, although the interviewer may be drinking one. Props like cigarettes and coffee cups will detract from your presentation.

3. *Remember, you're there to make an impression, not to entertain.* A light quip is fine, but don't ever risk telling jokes that might offend your interviewer.

Laughing at a joke is fine, but don't feel you need to "follow the leader." Becoming too familiar ultimately shows a lack of respect.

4. *Speak very carefully.* You may be faced with an interviewer who insists upon bringing up controversial topics to play devil's advocate. This interviewer is trying to test your reasoning skills. Defend your position objectively, rather than argumentatively. Never allow the debate to become a confrontation.

5. *Be careful of arrogance.* It's one thing to be self-confident and self-assured, it's another to be arrogant. It's a fine line to walk, because you'll be tooting your own horn—stress your positive qualities and accomplishments, but don't appear "holier-than-thou."

What Kinds of Questions Can You Expect?

The kinds of questions you may receive can range from college essay-like questions to very straightforward questions. At a recent Wharton interview, a prospective MBA was asked, "When you walk into a bookstore, what section do you head for?" and "If you had a chance to eat dinner with any distinguished person of your choice, who would that person be?" Let's take a look at these and other possible interview questions.

"Tell me a bit about yourself."

"What else would you like the admissions committee to know about you that has not been covered in your application?"

You can count on these two questions being asked, so you must be ready. Prepare in the fashion discussed earlier. They are rough questions because they are so vague, and they are meant to catch the unprepared off guard. What should you say? What should you omit? What does the interviewer want to know?

Use this opportunity to summarize your positive qualities and to convey your major theme and general impression. This is your chance to broaden and deepen the interviewer's knowledge of you. Remember, this is a marketing problem, so sell, sell, sell!

"Why do you want to attend this particular MBA program?"

Here's where your homework will pay off. It is impressive to have specific knowledge of the program, the curriculum, and the faculty, and to have specific reasons for wanting to be admitted to the school. Chances are you'll have answered this question in your essays, depending upon the school. Some reasons might include noted faculty (be specific), location, and special programs that interest you. The more specific, the better.

"What other schools are you applying to?"

Watch it here. Feel free to answer honestly if you wish, but don't run off a list of 20 schools that runs the gamut from Harvard to the local city graduate program. The recommendation is to mention a focused group of three or four. Mention schools that are roughly on a par with this particular program, since you don't want to mention a school that is either well above or well below this particular MBA school. You don't want to make this school appear as a consolation prize if you are not admitted to a much more prestigious school; you also don't want to show that this college is your "reach" or "dream" school. Subtly let the interviewer know that your intent is to attend one of the mentioned schools—if not this school, one of the others.

> "Who are your heroes, contemporary or historical?"
>
> "Name a person who has had a very important influence on you."
>
> "If you could spend time with any person—living, dead, or fictional—whom would you select, and why?"

This is a tough question, but a good one, because it allows for individuality in that every interviewee will make his or her own choice. You'll be remembered for your choice, so make it a good one. Use the word "hero" loosely—it doesn't have to be someone famous. It doesn't have to be a business leader (Lee Iacocca is a well-worn answer, and not too imaginative). Your choice will say a lot about who you are, so take your time, think long and hard about who you'd really want to spend time with, or who you really admire, and why.

> "What book have you read that is of great significance to you?"
>
> "What is your favorite book, and why?"
>
> "What section of the bookstore do you head for first?"

> "What magazines and/or newspapers do you read regularly?"
>
> "What is your favorite movie or TV show?"

This genre of question also allows for much individuality, and you should welcome the chance to set yourself apart from the other potential acceptees. They are designed to find out a bit more about your habits and hobbies and interests, those that weren't covered in the application. Don't repeat anything you might have mentioned in your essays. Steer clear of hokey answers—be honest about your choices, and be prepared to discuss the writer and format of books, magazines, and newspapers. Be aware of their thrust and theme, be it political or literary in nature. Be prepared to discuss your choice of television show or movie—why is it your favorite?

> "Describe a national or international issue of concern to you. Why does it concern you?"
>
> "What has been the most significant political or social movement of the twentieth century? Why?"
>
> "How do you feel about an issue in current events: nuclear arms race, abortion, drugs, gun control, etc.?"
>
> "What is the world's biggest problem, and what do you advocate for its solution?"

This last question actually used to appear on the Wharton application as an essay question. Be prepared to talk about current issues in the news, as these questions are meant to test your knowledge of the world around you and how you see yourself fitting into it. The most formidable part of these questions is selecting the issue. Use your colleagues and friends as sounding boards. Watch Sunday morning debate programs, and ABC's "Nightline." If you are knowledgeable about a specific area, this is the time to exhibit your competence. Most importantly, you must have well-thought-out points of view about the world around you. This is crucial, because it shows that you are a mature, aware, and socially conscious person. Defend your points of view with logical argumentation. These questions will allow you the opportunity to once again assert your individuality and intelligence. Welcome the opportunity to express yourself. If these or any other of the above questions completely throw you at this point, perhaps you should reconsider interviewing at a top business program. All successful candidates will be able to verbalize excellent responses to each one of these questions.

As a final question, you may be asked if *you* have any questions about the school. If you are not asked, make sure that you have two or three good questions ready anyway, and ask them. This shows that you've done your homework and have a true interest in the program. Again, make sure the questions are not covered in the catalogue. On the other hand, try to make sure the questions you have can be answered by the interviewer—don't play "stump the interviewer." Examples of questions might include: Will you be adding any new majors, courses, professors, programs, or clubs? What are the opportunities for employment while at school? Are you expecting any changes in recruiting this year?

Conclusion

The interview can be helpful or harmful to you, depending on your preparation and verbal communication abilities. Most people welcome interviews because they feel they can present themselves much better in person than on paper. If the guidelines in this chapter are followed, your interviews should be nothing short of successful!

11

Once You're In

Don't read this chapter until you've completed all of your applications, interviews, and have heard from at least one school! With a bit of luck, you'll have been accepted to a school of your choice. Now what? Now it's decision-making time.

The first thing you'll encounter is a tuition deposit. Most schools ask for a deposit to accompany an acceptance. Make sure before you accept an offer of admission that you really want to go to that school. If you haven't heard from your top-choice school, try to delay as long as possible. If you are forced to make a choice, then pick the next-best school and send in your deposit. The MBA application process has been an expensive one. If you get accepted to your first-choice school at a later date, you can forfeit the deposit and just think of it as another MBA application expense. At least you're assured of a place in one of the schools to which you applied.

In the best of all possible worlds, you will be accepted at all the schools to which you applied. Then, if you're undecided, you might want to think about the costs involved with each school. If one school offers you a better financial aid package than another, perhaps that's where you should go—provided, of course, that the schools are equal in reputation. Paying full price at Stanford is a better deal in the long run than going free to a local undistinguished program.

Reputation should be the first test you apply in making the final choice. Obviously, most people go to the best school they can get into. But given several schools with top national reputations, cost and location are the next factors that go into the decision. A final factor might be the desire to be with other students who are similar in background and abilities to you. If your quantitative skills are strong, you may want to work with other people who approach problems in a quantitative way. This may be the difference in attending Sloan over Harvard, for example.

The decision among several offers of admission is difficult—but as decisions go, it's a nice one to be able to make. The more painful decision is what to do if you are rejected by the MBA programs you feel are best for you. Basically, you have two choices: regroup, find out why you were rejected, correct the problem, and reapply; or apply to lesser-rank schools where you have a better chance for acceptance. (Not getting an MBA is not an option for readers of this book. Recall that all of the comments herein have been made assuming the reader is committed to an MBA career path. In other words, if the MBA was right for you when you started the application process, then it is right for you even if you've been initially rejected. If you feel that you don't want to pursue an MBA any longer, then you really didn't think about your future thoroughly in the first place.)

As you begin the reapplication process, it's important that you don't make the same mistakes twice. So your first step should be to try to find out *why* you were rejected. Quite often a friendly admissions staff member will tell you the reasons for your rejection. If you can't find out, read this book again very carefully with your applications in hand! Weigh the advice given against what you see on your application as objectively as you can, or get someone else to do it for you. Do any discrepancies come to mind? It may be that you didn't adhere to word limits, for instance, or that you weren't specific enough in supporting your assertions.

It may be that you simply applied too soon. This is the most common reason for rejection at the top schools—you did not have enough practical business experience (again, a minimum of three years) to impress the admissions committee. The solution to this problem is quite easy: Wait a year or two and reapply! If you are stuck in a routine job that you cannot leave, then volunteer for an interesting community service project. You already know the type of experience the selective MBA programs are looking for, so get involved in work that will give you that experience.

If you conclude that you were rejected because of a poor undergraduate record or low GMAT scores (unlikely at the top schools), then enroll in some part-time graduate courses, especially in business-related courses. The investment will improve your ability to function in a business school curriculum, and the good grades you earn will help convince the admissions committee that your undergraduate grades do not represent your current level of ability.

Again, though, your rejection is likely to hinge on your work experience and how you present yourself in the essays, particularly at the top programs. This might be a good time to reappraise your current situation. Are there opportunities for you to assume more authority in your present job? Are there more creative approaches you could use in problem solving? Can you tighten up your essays? If the answer is yes, then do it!

Conclusion

Hopefully this book has been helpful to you in your quest to gain acceptance to a selective MBA program. Chances are better than good that you've been accepted to one of your choice schools by this point. If so, congratulations! You're off to an exciting and rewarding experience! If not, don't give up—reread this book and try your hand again. You'll get in when you reapply, that's all. Good luck!

APPENDIX A

APPLICATION FILE TRACKER

NAME OF SCHOOL _____

ADDRESS _____

TELEPHONE # (ADMISSIONS OFFICE) _____

CONTACT PERSON (DIRECTOR OF ADMISSIONS) _____

APPLICATION FEE _____

Completed

____ Request School Catalog & Application

____ Photocopy All Forms

____ Arrange to Receive Transcripts

School _____

School _____

____ Arrange for GMAT Scores to Be Sent

____ Set Target Date of Application Completion   Date _____

____ Request Letters from Recommenders

____ Mail Supporting Material to Recommenders

____ Call Recommenders to Ensure Completion

____ Type and Complete Final Form and Essays

____ Mail Application (Return Receipt Requested, Certified)

____ Arrange for Interview (if Required or Desired)

____ Notification of Completed File Received

Directions: Place a copy of this form in each of your application folders, and check off your progress as you complete each item.

APPENDIX B

LETTERS OF RECOMMENDATION ORGANIZER

Recommender #1 (Academic)

Name _____ Title _____

Mailing Address _____ City _____ State _____

Zip Code _____ Telephone # _____

Materials to be sent in support _____
_____
_____

Recommender #2 (Professional)

Name _____ Title _____

Mailing Address _____ City _____ State _____

Zip Code _____ Telephone # _____

Supporting Material, if needed _____
_____
_____

Recommender #3 (if required or desired; Character Reference, Alumnus)

Name _____ Title _____

Mailing Address _____ City _____ State _____

Zip Code _____ Telephone # _____

Supporting Material, if needed _____

_____

_____

Directions: Use this form, or one like it of your own design, to keep track of your recommenders. If your recommenders vary from school to school, then place one of these sheets, along with your Application File Tracker, in each of your folders.

APPENDIX C

RELEVANT READING MATERIAL

ON MBA PROGRAMS

Curry, Boykin and Brian Kesbar, (eds.) *Essays That Worked for Business School.* Mustang Publishing, 1987. ($8.95)

Fischgrund, Tom, ed. *The Insider's Guide to the Top Ten Business Schools,* 3rd Ed. Little, Brown & Co., 1988. ($9.95)

Gourman, Jack. *The Gourman Report—A Rating of Graduate and Professional Programs,* 5th Ed. National Education Standards, 1988. ($14.95)

Miller, Eugene. *Barron's Guide to Graduate Business Schools,* 6th Ed. Barron's Educational Series, 1988. ($12.95)

The Official Guide to MBA Programs, 1988–90 Ed., Princeton, N.J.: Educational Testing Service, 1988. ($9.95)

ON THE MBA CAREER

Bronstein, Eugene, and Robert Hirsch. *The MBA Career—Moving on the Fast Track to Success.* Barron's Educational Series, 1983. ($6.95)

Careers and the MBA, 1989 Ed. Bob Adams Publishing, 1989. ($14.95)

Salzman, Marian, and Nancy Marx. *MBA JOBS!—An Insider's Guide to the Companies that Hire MBAs.* American Management Association, 1986. ($10.95)

STUDY GUIDES

Jaffe, Eugene, and Stephen Hilbert. *Barron's How to Prepare for the GMAT,* 7th Ed. Barron's Educational Series, 1989. ($9.95)

Martinson, Thomas, and David Ellis. *Arco's GMAT Preparation,* 4th Ed. Simon & Schuster, 1989. ($10.95)

The Official Guide for GMAT Review. Educational Testing Service, 1989. ($9.95)

Strunk & White, *Elements of Style,* 3rd Ed. MacMillan, 1979. ($4.95)

APPENDIX D

PERSONAL DATA FILE

As discussed in Chapter 7, all of the applications and essays require detailed factual information. Beyond those requirements, however, are areas of your life that you should attempt to recall as well. Use this Personal Data File to start listing this information. Follow the suggestions in Chapter 7 regarding the use of this information.

Personal Data
Full name
Address
Phone number
Mother's full name
Address
Father's name
Address
Date of birth
Race
Creed
National origin
Sex
Marital status
Parental status
Military status
Economic status
Health
Disabilities, if any

Achievements
Hobbies
Travel
Sports
Publications
Patents
Independent research
Languages spoken
Languages read or understood
Computer languages

Musical instruments
Special skills (such as CPR)
Licenses held
Recent reading
Sports

Activities
Community Service Organizations
— elective offices held
— special projects
— honors or awards
Professional Organizations
— elective offices held
— committees chaired
— papers or projects
— honors or awards
Political offices held or campaigned for

Academic Background
HIGH SCHOOL
— address
— years of attendance
— type of diploma
— sports activities
— extracurricular activities
— academic interests or honors
— nonacademic honors
— class rank

COLLEGE OR UNIVERSITY
  — address
  — years of attendance
  — degree earned
  — graduation honors
  — major subject
  — GPA in major subject
  — minor subject, if any
  — competitive sports
  — extracurricular activities
  — academic awards
  — nonacademic awards or honors
  — thesis topic, if required
  — GPA
  — class rank
  — favorite courses
  — professors with whom you had a close association

Postgraduate Courses, Degrees, and Training Programs
Name of institution
Type of course or program
Degree earned, if any
Professional Certificate awarded
Years of attendance
Grades
Names of professors
Professional licenses held